THE ESSENCE OF A WOMAN

Bold, Beautiful and Resilient

By K. N. Vaughn

PUBLISHING

The Essence of a Woman

Copyright © 2021 K. N. Vaughn

All rights reserved. No part of this publication may be reproduced, stored in a retrieval system, or transmitted in any form or by any means – for example, electronic, mechanical, photocopying, recording or any other – except for brief quotations in printed reviews – without the prior written permission of the author.

Published in Great Britain by:

SelectArrow Ltd.
www.selectarrow.net

ISBN: 978-1-7398830-0-3

Cover and interior design: Homer Slack
Editor: Angela Slack

ACKNOWLEDGEMENTS

I would like to thank my mother for providing emotional support for this book 'The Essence of a Woman,' to come to fruition and for always being there, loving me unconditionally and molding me into the woman I am today.

I also want to thank my daughter for putting up with me throughout the arduous process of writing this book and just for being the ambitious, loving, strong, young lady that she has blossomed into.
I want to acknowledge all my family members who helped me along the way, my sister, my aunt and father who passed away 4 years ago. You all played a part in my life and helped me to get where I am today and for that I am grateful.

ENDORSEMENT

This book is definitely an inspiration to all people seeking strength, encouragement and guidance to break free from abusive and toxic relationships or to help them fully recover from one. Whether male or female we are not immune to being victims of narcissistic individuals. That's why this book is so important because it educates you on what to look for in those individuals, so you don't fall into their trap.

Narcissists prey on people who they think are weak but in reality, they are strong, empathetic people who take their abuse and still try to find goodness in their wicked ways. This book will give you the tools you need for proper discernment and to be just as Jesus said: *"Behold, I send you forth as sheep in the midst of wolves: be ye therefore wise as serpents and harmless as doves."*

I recommend K. N.Vaughn's, **The Essence of A Woman,** as a well-needed source of wisdom.

Morlon Greenwood,
Former 8 year starting linebacker (Miami Dolphins & Houston Texans),
President of the NFL Alumni, Las Vegas Chapter.
CEO of MG52 Foundation.

ENDORSEMENT

I have known Karen for several years and I must say she's one of the most loving and down-to-earth women I have ever met. Her pleasant spirit is a testament to her strong emotional intelligence. She's like a quiet storm, a woman who has traveled life's journey and witnessed some trying times and has overcome them. She's the right one to help other women see their value and worth.

Karen is one of a kind and knows it, yes she has found herself and walks boldly as a woman in touch with herself. As I say in my poem entitled, 'The Inner Woman', "There is another side to the moon, so it is with the woman, just believe..." In this book, Karen helps women to reconnect with their feminine selves and to accept the beauty of being unapologetically a woman. I'm very proud of you, lady.

Dr. J.A. Salaam,
Personal and Professional Development Trainer

ENDORSEMENT

K.N.Vaughn's, **The Essence Of A Woman,** deserves to be on the top of the pile of required reading in this genre, for its honesty and well-needed fresh take on a women's role in the world. She has written a biographical prescription to women, a recommended text that is authoritatively put forward, to women especially, who like herself, have found themselves victims of domestic abuse. She has given a very empathetic but firm instruction manual for getting out safely or even better for avoiding the pitfall altogether.

As a man, it was most gratifying to read a modern woman's story of triumph over adversity that was not poisoned with acrimony and gender bias towards men in general. This is noteworthy from a woman of the Afro-Caribbean diaspora, as in recent times such women have projected very hardened personas. She came out of her traumatic circumstances without losing herself. Yes, she did not swap her femininity for a coat of armor in place of what makes her quintessentially feminine; thereby dispelling the common myth that to be a feminine woman means being weak and naive.

There are still men who are looking for feminine women - they love the essence of a woman- her boldness, her beauty and resilience and that is what this book is seeking to preserve. In response, I say wholeheartedly, bring it on ladies and bravo Karen!

Dr. Norman Whyte,
Mental Health, PhD

FOREWORD

She's a mother, a daughter, a sister, a friend and a woman of courage. I say courage because Karen has written a book that was born from her life experiences and provides an inspirational and honest testimony to which readers of her first book will relate.

Karen speaks clearly about how necessary it is for women to understand their uniqueness in society and how important it is for them to be able to know themselves well. Karen would like for women to get a clear identity of themselves, evolve and be courageous enough to take the steps to improve themselves. Karen pours her heart into writing The Essence of a Woman, her first book. She explores and brings to the forefront the need for women to become very aware of obvious signs, good or bad, so that when dating, they can make better decisions prior to any possible relationship.

Karen delves into her journey of motherhood and how her children help to define who she is today. In all of Karen's personal struggles in life, her personal faith in God seems to have been an anchor for her to rely on no matter what she faced.
The Essence of a Woman is a book written for men and women as all can learn from her written words. I feel very assured of that. Let's get you reading! You will enjoy it!

Milton McCulloch
Author/Poet/Playwright/Songwriter.

INTRODUCTION

I wrote this book because I strongly believe we all need to reconnect with our inner being and realize that we have the power of choice to determine our own destiny; that is, if we choose to cooperate with the plans that our Creator has for us then we will definitely come out victorious. I would like everyone to take a look at their lives and realize that whatever they have encountered on their journey through life has helped to mold them and has allowed them to become more resilient. I can attest to this especially having gone through a rough 2020 and 2021 having experienced a global pandemic for the first time.

As women, we particularly need to realize that we are strong and we can overcome all difficulties or obstacles that come our way, once we rely on our faith and foundation values. We sometimes find that our womanhood is tested especially if we encounter trials and tribulations in our lives but how we are able to respond to these adversities and become a better woman is what makes us stronger.

This book is written to inspire those who feel overwhelmed by obstacles or adversities in their lives; I am here to say don't despair, you are on your way to becoming a better woman. I have shared with you what has made me stronger. I have outlined how you can respond appropriately and effectively to the following challenges: 1. Feelings of inadequacy and unworthiness. 2. Depression and Anxiety. 3. Juggling Marriage, Children and a Career and lastly, How to Become a Better You.

I am confident that these tips mentioned above will help you to live bold, beautiful and resilient lives.
Chin up and let's get going,

Karen

TABLE OF CONTENTS

1. Identifying Yourself 1

2. Establishing Relationships 15

3. Motherhood 27

4. Marriage 37

5. Raising Children 47

6. Financial Problems 53

7. Invest in Yourself 59

8. Are You Your Types' Type? 63

9. Stronger Now 75

CHAPTER 1

Who Are You?

This looks like the most straightforward question anybody can ask you. A five-year-old today could provide a few answers to the question. It is simple and basic but in reality, most people do not know who they are and in turn fail to realize what they want from life. **You have to be familiar with yourself to be able to know what your needs are.** I have been asked this question countless times when I was younger and I always had a ready and simple answer to give. "I am Karen and I am the only child of my mother. I do not know my father because he died when I was three years old. Simple!"

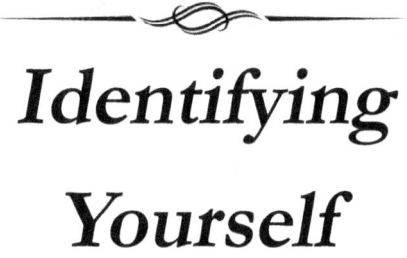

I stuttered when a close friend of mine, Cheryl, asked me this question when I ran away from my husband. "Who are you?" She said. I burst into tears and tried to find my words. It was at that moment I realized I had lost my identity long before I knew. Nobody can love you if you do not love yourself! Identifying yourself and acknowledging that you exist as a person, because God created you to be a wonderful creation and not a duplicate of someone else is one of the best decisions you can ever make in life. **My key principle**

in life is self respect and respect for others. This principle has influenced my life so much it has made me a better person. When you respect yourself, you show love to yourself because you understand that you are unique and the world does not get to have two of you. Leave a legacy in someone else's life before you leave because we are all pilgrims on a journey on Earth. Some people's journeys get cut off instantly, others in later years. You cannot know who is going to outlive who, so love yourself and love others while you are able to.

Who Am I?
I grew up as an only child of my mother and I watched my mother grow into a strong wonderful woman. She played a huge role in my life as a father and a mother, I am indeed very grateful for that. I did not have much while growing up because my mum worked at a launderette and she did not have much to give out. She started working two jobs when I turned five to provide for my basic needs. She wanted me to become the best I could be and in her words, "You are not mediocre and I do not want the world to make a mediocrity out of you!" I failed three subjects in fourth grade and I was scared to tell my mom. My mom spoke and acted smartly all the time and I did not want her to think that she gave birth to a dummy because I felt I was a dummy.

"Were there children who passed?" She asked me when I finally got the courage to tell her.
"Yes, Tommy got the highest score in all three of them."
"Who is Tommy?" She asked.
"A boy in my class."

It was around Christmas time, my mom held my shoulders and said some things to me. She was the first and only person to have ever told me that. "I gave birth to you alone, Karen! Nobody else but one

Karen. I do not know who Tommy is but he better get ready because you are about to outshine him!"

I did not outshine Tommy the way my mom wanted me to, but my grades improved and I soon came among the top six in my class. I only started to take charge of my life when I realized that I came into this world alone and I owe it to myself and God to make the best out of my life. The mistake many women make is not having a personal identity before marriage or losing their identity after marriage. If you know your identity as a woman, nobody can ever destroy you! I lost track of this when I got married and I am thankful that I have gotten back to my foundation principles and nobody can destroy me anymore.

When building a connection with a loved one, do not lose your identity midcourse. When I first met my ex-husband, I was overwhelmed with the thought that I was now in a relationship. It was a fascinating experience for me and I found myself losing my identity as the relationship progressed.

What Does it Mean to Lose Oneself?
You lose yourself when you no longer know who you are. You lose yourself when you begin to doubt your existence. Anyone can lose themselves at any stage in their life. It could happen when you make new friends and you begin to act more like your new friends and less like yourself. When you find yourself in a new romantic relationship, it is quite possible to lose yourself to your partner. You become too absorbed in the relationship and at most times, it can be difficult to notice it. My ex-husband fascinated me. He was everything I always wanted to be. Smart, rich and successful in business. I did not know this until it was too late, but I began to bend my values and faith to suit his. My story is familiar to someone

you know, right? Or perhaps, to you? This is the reality many women face. We lose ourselves and time passes by, then one day reality hits home and we realize that the relationship is over and then we begin to ask ourselves "What happened to me?" "How did I get here?"

What was my identity outside of being a mother and a wife, I needed to reinstate myself. Is that a bad thing? There is nothing wrong with being excited about being a wife and a mother or getting married and having a family. Even the Bible says "He who finds a wife, finds a good thing." However, does that mean that all marriages are successful? Marriage is a beautiful thing, but not everyone is designed for that. If you don't know your identity in life, then you should think twice. Should I have taken that route? No! I had an identity that I held on to originally but it seems as if I lost it along the way. It is a dangerous thing to get married to someone who belittles you to the point where you lose your identity.

In any type of relationship, it is normal to admire or adopt certain habits from your loved ones. It becomes a problem when you begin to morph into them and get to the point that you stop acting like yourself!

How Do You Know If You Are Losing Yourself?

- You can no longer recognize your goals, aspirations and passion; this is very deadly. You go into the relationship with the belief that you are going to grow and blossom but then you get crushed. Your purpose in life takes a back seat and you feel lifeless.
- You cannot stand for yourself. Have you been in a type of relationship where it seems like your opinions do not matter; you cannot speak up because you are shut down every time or nobody pays attention to anything you say?

- Your life is monotonous and it follows the same pattern. You do the same thing over and over again. Wake up - Kids - Clean - Kids - Clean - Sex! Your quality time is non-existent and although you love your family, you want something outside of this repetitive cycle.
- You are stuck in the past; you have accepted your life for what it is but your thoughts are stuck in what is already gone. You keep thinking about what the future would have been if you had done things differently. It is as if you had been sleeping with the enemy all along.

Is Marriage the Enemy?
Marriage is a beautiful institution created by God. It is the union between a man and a woman who come together to become one. A home based on love and God should not be divided. The husband should complement the wife and the wife should complement the husband. It takes two people to work towards achieving a successful marriage. If only one party is willing to put in all the work, the marriage is doomed to fail.

Marriage can be the enemy if you want it to be. I got married and I became solely defined by my relationship status. I became so absorbed into my wifely and motherly duties that I forgot why I existed in the first place. I watched my ex-husband pursue his dreams and he told me to put my dreams on hold because I was a wife and mother now. My marriage was nothing like I envisioned it to be. It was not the happily ever after I wished for and at some point, I wished I never got married.

God has called every one of us to use the gifts that we were all born with, but if you do not know what you are called to be, then it really is pointless. Marriage plays a huge role in a married woman's life and it is a huge part of her identity, but not all of who she is. If you get married to the wrong person, marriage can be a curse and if you get married to the right person marriage can be a blessing. I got married at a very young age. The age of me finding myself and understanding who I was supposed to become in life. I got married at an age where I was naïve and this made me susceptible to manipulation. I realized very quickly that when you do decide to get married you should choose someone who will love you, uplift you and watch you grow.

Men and women should enter into marriage with their own identities. If a man gets married without figuring out who he is, it could pose a great danger to the union and become a threat to the family later down the line. If you have the right mentality, you may encounter fewer problems. By that I mean, if you are the type of person who is teachable and introspective then you may not make as many mistakes and you can quickly correct the ones you have made. Every marriage has its ups and down and no marriage is perfect. Never be deceived by peoples' false persona and the facade of a perfect relationship. Nobody knows what goes on behind closed doors, so be careful and prepared before you take that step. This is your life.

The Identity of Being Female
Let us talk about what being a woman is all about and how society views womanhood.
What it means to be a woman has many meanings depending on culture. Connotations surrounding being a woman go beyond stereotypes, biology and hormones. One of my friends told me something one beautiful morning and it stuck with me and I am going to share this with you. She said that being a woman meant that we as humans are defined by our accomplishments and what we define as being successful. Hear me out, my friend didn't say that biology, hormones and stereotypes do not contribute to what makes

us women, but they shouldn't define who we are. What do I mean by that? Society and the world we live in has attributed marriage as the climax of a woman's success. It does not matter if she owns a number of businesses or if she has a lot of money. If she is not married yet and has no husband and children society still considers her unsuccessful as a woman!

I watched this happen to my mother. She lost my father two years after marriage and it took her years to recover. She refused to marry and she remained a single mother until the day she died. Many people did not know her story or where she was coming from. Many assumed she was a divorcee or somebody who hated men. Imagine having people make assumptions about you before getting to know you. My mother will forever be a mentor to me and I admired her right from when I was a kid. She was a strong woman and as time passed by, she grew stronger and she was so full of wisdom. I watched her while growing up and at times, she made decisions that didn't make sense to me, but as I grew older, I got to understand the pearls of wisdom in her decisions.

My mother taught me what it meant to be a wife and a mother. She taught me how to stand for myself and fight for the truth. She taught me what it felt like to love and be loved, but somehow along the way, I forgot everything she taught me when I got married. It became difficult to stand up for myself. I do not subscribe to the teaching that says that before anything else, women are mothers and wives. I believe that I am a human being before anything else and I should be treated with love and respect.

Fighting Stereotypes
Stereotypes could be true for a particular thing or group of people, but it does not represent the entire population of that thing or group

of people. It would be a fallacy to say that **X** did this which means that the entire population acts like **X**. I can conclude that there is no clear way to define who a woman is. Stereotypes give you a false idea about the environment around you and this can make you prejudiced towards people and groups. Stereotyping men and women have been seen as a normal thing to do in today's world. Some stereotypes about women include;

- Women are terrible drivers.
- Women are talkative.
- Women only date rich men.
- Women are obsessed with their looks.
- Women are lazy.
- Women are too emotional.
- Women are jealous beings.
- Women hate women.

Some women behave like this, but you cannot judge the entire population of women in the world based on what you have witnessed from a number of women. Not every woman is jealous of another woman. That is just ridiculous! Not all women are lazy! Mind you, we have lazy men too!

Our identities come from who we are and how we view ourselves. Our genes play a role in creating who we are but our personalities are also formed and influenced by many social and cultural influences over some time. However, what does God want us to become? It is a significant part of our existence to realize that God has a purpose for every one of us and it is left for us to discover what our innate desires are. Some people do not discover what they want early in life while others discover it later in life. Pray and trust God to lead you to the path He has designed for you.

I remember having this passion inside of me while growing up and I knew that I wanted something different in life. I wanted to become a writer to encourage people and let them know there is more to life than just existing. Life is complex and it is our identity in Christ that makes us scale through life's challenges. My mom bought me books to read and I was [still am] a lover of books. Flipping through the pages of a book and breathing in the scent of the pages excited me. I knew that I was going to be a writer someday and that I was going to inspire and encourage others, but it was a question of how and when?

When I got married, it seemed as if that day would never come to pass. The fire in me began to fade as time passed by and I became scared that one day, my children would grow up and leave me alone. I also feared being left alone with a man who did not love me. What was worse, I had no dreams to keep me alive. It was scary but every day that I woke up, I believed that someday I was going to achieve my dreams because I knew that God was not done with me yet.

Marriage is a blessing if you have figured yourself out and you can maintain your individuality. Do not lose track of your values, beliefs, faith, passion and goals. Do not pretend to agree with your partner when you truly disagree or go along with things you do not believe in. Sadly, I had lost my identity in my marriage, I looked to my ex-husband to fulfill all my needs and when he didn't, I was left devastated and angry. The problem lies in the fact that women are tied down and this is attributed to men; and this suggests that marriage should be the ultimate destination for all women. What happens when this theory does not apply to all women? What happens when some women do not find a suitable partner in the first place or they found a suitable partner but he left? In my case, I believed I found someone good enough, at least I thought I did but he was not who I thought he was!

Becoming a Wife

I got married when I was nineteen. It was a scary moment for me and I thought that it was what I wanted. I was convinced that I had made the right decision. Alas, I was not thinking with my head and I allowed my emotions to consume me. I met the man I thought was the love of my life just about when I was applying to colleges. It looked like everything was working together and falling into place. I had met the love of my life and I was going to college, double blessings for me. I was swept off my feet by the way he spoke and carried himself. Where I came from I was not exposed to many men like him or I failed to pay any attention to them. My thinking was that since I had applied to study business in various colleges outside of Miami and I met a man who worked as an entrepreneur and a business strategist, I believed God had delivered my blessings in a shiny package. Unfortunately, we all know that not all that glitters is gold.

Do not get deceived by outward appearances. They may appear so glittery that they block your vision, therefore you get distracted and cannot see what is really underneath. Shiny packages can be deceptive, they disrupt your emotions, you lose your focus, lower your guard and you get caught. Remember the world is made up of all different types of people. We may believe these people are 'God-sent;' they may be handsome, tall, well dressed, eloquent speakers and so you may feel as though they are the total package. However, remember this is someone you are hoping to spend the rest of your life with; It's not the outer but the inner appearance that really matters. Never become blinded by what you see in front of you, look deeper within.

While being in a relationship with him, I waited impatiently to get answers from the colleges I applied to. I guess the anxiety was the reason I ignored so many red flags in the relationship. I would bring up my desire to attend college and express how apprehensive I was about waiting and he would brush it off like I hadn't said anything important at all. We courted for six months and he asked me to marry him and I told him delightedly, yes. I wasn't in college yet and I was about to get married to the love of my life and it felt like I knew what I was doing. My mom was against it and she told me to relax and think my decision through, but I didn't. I was happy with him and that was all that mattered.

Getting Married at a Young Age

Marriages end and couples get divorced irrespective of how young or how old they got married. Everything boils down to their understanding of marriage and how they view each other. If you see your husband as a friend, partner, lover, helper, as a potentially good father for your future children and he sees you as the same, I think that there will be a huge difference in the marriage. Maturity generally comes with age but needless to say, not all adults are mature. That does not mean that two teenagers getting married today are mature, they still have a lot of things to discover about the world and themselves. I on the other hand got married when I thought I was ready, but I wasn't. It didn't help that I married someone who wasn't ready to help me grow.

I got married during the period I got accepted to study business at Barry University in Miami. I was excited and I couldn't wait to tell my mom and husband the good news. My mom was glad I was going to college even though she was not in support of me getting married at that young age. She was happy for me and she prayed for me. I told my ex-husband the good news with the same energy that I had told my mother. I remember vividly how his expression was grim. He didn't laugh or smile or do anything. He just stared at me like a ghost. I didn't know what to do. I had just told my newly wedded husband that I was going to college and he didn't respond. I called my mom that evening and told her what happened and she told me to be patient, that he was in shock and was yet to process the good news. So I waited patiently. The next morning, he called me and sat me down and told me that he didn't think I needed to go to college. In his words, "You're a wife now and you may soon become a mother. College can wait!" That was enough to stop my career.

College Can Wait!

I was confused. When we dated he had told me he did not want to wait for me to finish college and he wanted to get married to me as soon as possible."We will get married and you will go to college. I will take care of all the bills and we will have a maid who will assist in the home," he said.

We agreed that I was not going to have kids until I was done with college because it was not going to be easy for us as a family if I went to school at the same time. That was what I had told my mom and she agreed reluctantly and I entered into the marriage with that belief but it was all a lie! We got married and he changed everything we ever talked about. I had kids and I did not go to college. He lied to me and I was stupid enough to have believed all that he said.

Defining the terms in a relationship is very important. Go into a relationship with confidence and not naivety. I wish I had done that before getting married. I was consumed with my ex-husband; while dating I became so naïve. I held him in such high esteem that I started to feel and act insecure. I let him dictate my life! Never allow another person to control your life, nobody is God!

Do Identities Matter?

We are God's greatest creation! We are all loved and blessed by God.

Don't go looking for a man or woman to complete you because that is too much weight and pressure to put on another human being. People that go into marriages, without having a clear identity and focus in life, hoping that partners will fulfill those desires will always be left disappointed. You are not an incomplete person and if you have been having that thought, I think it is time for you to do away with such thoughts. You are enough!

When you are in a relationship, try to be as realistic as possible. Most people enter marriages with expectations and when these expectations are not met by their partner, they become hurt and resentful. Mostly, these expectations are fantasies and they give you false hope. When you have these unreasonable expectations, they ruin your idea of a partner.

- **Do not expect your partner to have the same values as you.** Remember that getting into a relationship means that you and your partner are coming from two different backgrounds. Hence, you carry your values and expectations into the relationship. The fact that you and your partner may not have the same values will become a point of frustration and will require effort from both parties.
- **Do not expect your partner to automatically know how to please you.** If you expect your partner to do things and there is no communication, it can pose a lot of damage to the relationship. Your partner is not a mind reader! If you want things to be done, communicate with them.
- **Do not expect your partner to change for you.** If you go into a relationship with the expectation of changing each other it will only lead to disaster. Your partner is already grown and it will be difficult to start to change an adult. Changing your partner leads to your partner losing themselves and except they are causing

harm to you and your family, do not expect to change your partner. It is important to share interests in a relationship but it is also important to have your autonomy.

- **Never enter into a relationship hoping the relationship will work itself out.** Both partners should be prepared to put the necessary work into the relationship. Be prepared to listen to each other and be attentive to each other's needs and wants.
- **Having high expectations of yourself.** Sometimes people get into relationships and they set high expectations for themselves. For instance, men feel that they have to live up to the expectations of the bedrock, protector and Mr. do and know it all in the family. Women also think that they have to run the home well and take care of the children. It may very well be that your partner is much better at this so be willing to come to reasonable arrangements based on each other's strengths.

CHAPTER 2

Establishing Relationships

As humans, we need to make sure we are establishing good relationships. Relationships are what make up a community. People do not work and exist in isolation. We all need to work together. We are social beings and we always want to create successful relationships with others. You have to understand what relationships are all about. What exactly is a relationship and why do we crave it? Contrary to popular belief, introverts are not exempted from relationships; platonic friendships, romantic relationships, or whatever 'ships' exist out there. Connecting with people around you is not a bad thing, rather it is healthy. A divorce shouldn't be a reason to stay away from people; to steer clear from having any form of relationship with people.

Defining Relationships

Defining relationships should not be a problem for women. We should learn how to discern those who value and respect us and those who are wasting our time. We should be able to define our relationships with the opposite sex in order to avoid any form of confusion. Do not let a man waste your time. Let him tell you where you stand in the relationship. Do not confuse texting and calling everyday with a relationship. If he has not asked you out yet or defined what is going on, then there is no relationship.

Do not let men string you along. If he wants to see you, he will make the time. If he wants a relationship, he will tell you. I have seen a lot of men do this. They tell you they want to see you, but do not make an effort to see you. He is seeing other women and wants to keep his options open in case it does not work out with the others. When a man is truly interested in you, he will ask you out! There is no need to ponder about these things. If he wants you, you will know.

Define your relationships and do not allow anyone to string you along. If men want you, they will fit you into their busy schedule. The same goes for women, if they want a man, they will fit him into their schedule. Don't be carried away with the things he tells you. If he calls you pet names as if he is your boyfriend but he is not your actual boyfriend, then he is just wasting your time.

After going through a divorce with my ex-husband, I met a man who was three years older than me. Let us call him Nick. He was sweet and caring and I liked him. I had just come out of a terrible marriage and my mind was already sharpened. I made a mistake once and I did not want to make another one. I paid close attention to what he said and what he did. What he said was in contrast to what he did and that bothered me a lot. He did not have respect for women and it clearly showed in the way he acted towards me. I told him about my two boys and he wanted to meet them.

"It will be fun to get to know all of you, including your boys," He said.
"I do not think it is wise to do that," I answered.
"Why not?" He replied.
"I do not want to," I stated firmly.
"But why?" He inquired
"I do not want you to." I insisted.
He got angry and walked out of the restaurant where we were having

our dinner. I was thirty years old then and I was in the process of finalizing my divorce from my ex-husband. It was not a tough process for me because we had been separated for years and he had completely forgotten about me and the boys. I knew this because my friends had told me they had seen him with several women when I left the matrimonial house.

"We saw him at the mall with a young girl. She could not be more than twenty-three." Barbara said. "Do not let that bother you," said Deborah. You dodged a bullet!"

It became evident that he had a fondness for young girls. Probably the lady was naïve just like I was when I first met him. I was not sad because he was with somebody else, but I was sad for him and her. I felt sorry for him because he needed girls way younger than himself to make him feel younger. I felt sorry for the lady who was falling into a trap that I was once stuck in.

So when I met the other man in my thirties. I had to be smarter than I was at nineteen. I had regained my identity and I was not prepared to lose it again. I did not let him get to my head and play me like a fool; so when I detected some red flags, I flew!

Red Flags

It is astonishing to admit but let me tell you that some women do not understand what a red flag is. They have heard people say things like, "there were red flags so I ran away," or "I can't believe I did not detect those red flags." If more and more women understood the concept of red flags, then we would not have many women in bad relationships.

Red flags are signals and indicators that a probable threat or problem is lurking around. A red flag simply means there is danger coming. Therefore, what do you do when a bomb is about to detonate, or a killer is on the loose? You run away and hide! You get away from the danger as soon as possible because you love and care about yourself. With that said, here are some common red flags:

- **Lack of or poor Communication-** a total lack of communication in a relationship is a red flag. If you struggle to have a sound relationship with the people with whom you spend time and work everyday, how much more difficult will it be to develop a romantic relationship without good communication? Some people have difficulty in expressing how they feel and this can be a huge problem in the relationship. Nobody is a mind reader! Nick was not honest and open and I could tell that he was not communicating properly with me. He would say some things and I would have to rack my brain to understand what exactly he meant. He did that intentionally. He would say a couple of things, that did not make any sense and I would be left pondering on those words.

- **Immaturity-** Wisdom does not come with maturity. Immaturity is a huge red flag when it comes to relationships. Immature adults have problems handling situations. These types of people are trouble! They find it difficult to handle situations like finances and personal space. Nick had terrible experiences with money and therefore he handled money irresponsibly. I did not know him for a long time but I was able to notice some of his bad attitudes/habits towards money. Immature people cannot hold a job and they do not have concrete plans for the future. Do not expect to have a solid relationship with people who do not have solid plans for their future.

- **Lingering feelings for an ex partner-** If your partner has not gotten over his ex, then this is going to be a problem. When he has unresolved issues with his past, he will have a problem dealing with the present and the future. Your partner could still be close to his ex, calls them often, hangs out with them. Or he may talk badly about his ex, blame his ex and all this means he is still hung up on his ex.

- **Knowing when you have reached your limit-** You should be able to detect when something becomes too much. How much is too much? If your partner criticizes everything you do and complains a lot, making it look like you cannot do things right, run! This can be tricky because most women are not able to detect this behavior. Sadly, this causes them to think that their partner is trying to help them grow and are unaware that they are being controlled. It is a problem when someone does not like the way you speak, eat, dress, or do anything in general. My ex-husband criticized everything I did even when he knew it was something I could not control. If you feel demeaned and humiliated, you have to call it quits. You are being emotionally abused.

- **Signs of manipulation and control-** If your partner wants to isolate you from the world, run! Some men can be like that. They want to keep you away from friends and family. Pay attention to this red flag. They complain about your friends, family, co-workers, or anybody who dares come closer to you. He will make it look like he is protecting you from bad people and this will make you want to trust him more. This manipulative tactic is smart because it makes you start to doubt your support system and then you are left with him, alone!

- **Signs of Anger Management Problems-** If your partner overreacts and loses his temper about little things, then it is time for you to break free from him. This shows that he has anger issues and is ready to flare up at any given opportunity.

Uncontrolled anger is a red flag in any kind of relationship. Anger is a natural emotion and everybody gets angry at some point in their life, but it only becomes a problem when one does not know how to control such emotions. While dating my ex-husband, he got angry about insignificant things. I did not think it was a problem, because I thought it was supposed to be like that. I never realized my mistake until he unleashed his anger on me physically. I was fortunate to get out, but for many it's too late. Take some time to really examine yourself against these red flag indicators and honestly determine if you are in a dangerous relationship and summon up the courage to plan your speedy escape.

The importance of friendships to single mothers?
Establishing friendships is very important. Before I got married, I had no challenges when it came to making new friends and maintaining my old friendships. It was something that happened instantaneously. And when I got married to my ex-husband, it seemed as if the entire world had taken the back seat and it was just my family and I. I poured out my body and soul into my marriage and one day, I woke up with no marriage and it was just me and my kids. Have you ever been in that kind of situation? Have you ever been the only single mom among your friends and then you felt so out of place that you gradually withdrew? You are not the only one out there, just as I was not the only one then, who felt that way. If you have ever felt that way, now is the time to change that!

I have met many single mothers who relegated themselves to the background because their partner left them and they did not know what else to do. So they shied away from their friends and families because of the divorce, forgetting the fact that it wasn't God's plan for them in the beginning. God doesn't want us as women to be in the background. Being a divorcee or a single mother shouldn't stop us from forming relationships with others.

Becoming a mother was difficult for me and it was a challenge. I am not ashamed to say that and I do not think anybody should be ashamed too. Nobody wants to talk about the difficulty of being a woman, becoming a mother and being a mother.

Years ago, women didn't have careers and they were tasked with the job of keeping the home and raising the children. Women who had jobs were mostly involved in 'feminine' jobs like seamstresses, nurses, teachers and maids. It was okay for women to take up these roles because we were told lies that those jobs were suitable for us because we were women. Today, the narrative has changed and it is still being changed.

I wasn't allowed to work when I got married and it was difficult for me because I had always envisioned myself working and doing the things that I love to do. I didn't think that I was going to be a housewife and it never occurred to me that it was ever going to happen to me. Being a housewife is not a problem, but it only becomes a problem when you have no intention of being one. I was forced to do it. I got admitted to study business and I dreamed that one day I was going to be in charge of my own business. When it became clear to me that my dream wasn't going to be realised, It was shocking and I remember crying so hard that I didn't want to eat. How can one man put a hold on someone else's life and think that it is okay to do that?

I didn't have many friends because I didn't go out often. I had no school to go to and I had no work to go to. I was stuck at home doing the same monotonous tasks everyday. Consequently, the more time I spent doing these things, the angrier I became. I wasn't pleased with myself and with my ex-husband. I would wake up in the morning with this bitterness in my heart and go to bed with the same bitterness. I was alone and needed somebody to talk to because my ex-husband was not always there.

In the early stages of our marriage, things changed drastically. I wasn't allowed to work so I had too much time on my hands. I tried connecting more with my husband, but he didn't want to connect with me. It was really hard to make friends because most of the friends I had weren't married yet and it felt strange being around them. They talked a lot about boys, parties and school. All I had was a failed marriage that was draining me emotionally, physically and spiritually. All this was enough for me to withdraw from them and it seemed that I wasn't missed that much.

Why Do Relationships Matter?

For me, it did. Friendships and creating relationships with others outside of marriage mattered a lot. If I had friends around me, my mental health would have been better back then. I believe relationships are an essential part of life and we should learn to embrace them even when we are married. It is good to have friends as an individual and it is also good to have friends as a couple. I knew I needed a relationship outside of my marriage but it was difficult for me to establish one. Most of the relationships I had were mostly from the events I attended with my ex-husband. I didn't relate so well with his work friends because I was way younger than they were and I felt awkward.

I had made a couple of friends and we usually met up once a week without our husbands' knowledge. I remember walking around in the mall searching for some baby stuff I thought I was going to need and a couple of ladies walked up to me and asked me friendly questions out of the blue. I was shocked because I wasn't expecting to make any friends. I rarely had friends around me, except when my ex-husband had guests in the house. Usually I would just sit and nod at whatever they discussed.

These ladies introduced me to something new and daring. Everyone felt welcomed in the group, the atmosphere was so tranquill, I was fascinated by them. We were more than friends and our relationship grew from friendships to sisterhood. We were seven in the group and two of us were the youngest. I was twenty-one at that time and the other lady, Alison, was twenty. I clicked with Alison immediately because we were the youngest and I could relate very much to her story. She had put her dreams on pause immediately after she got married to her husband too. She also did not envision her marriage to turn out that way.

Cheryl was the oldest member of our group. She was fifty years old. She worked in one of the most prominent law firms in Miami. She lost her husband to cancer when she was just thirty-two years old and she had raised her four kids all by herself. Cheryl was a woman of dignity and perseverance. I remember sitting across from Cheryl and it was not just her purple flowery blouse that caught my attention, it was her smile! She welcomed us with so much joy, she gave me hope.

"Hello, I'm Cheryl and I did not choose to be a single mother, but I have learned to love it anyway. I lost my husband at the age of thirty-two years and I have been a single mother for eighteen good years. It hurts every single time to think that I thought I was going to be with Pete for the rest of my life. It hurts more because you never know who outlives who. I pray to be there with my children until they no longer need me!"

I gawked at her and wondered what it was like for her to have carried such a weight of sorrow in her heart and yet she did not look like she had problems.

"What is your name?" She said to me. My heart pounded.
"Tell us a little more about yourself, don't be shy!"

What was I supposed to say? That I hated my marriage and wished that I never married? I felt like an awkward young girl with her baby, sitting uncomfortably amid matured women and I questioned myself whether I truly belonged.

"I am Karen and I am twenty-two years old. I got married when I was nineteen and I wish I never did."
"Why?" They asked.
"It is nothing like what I envisioned it to be. I was happy before I got married and now I am living in misery."

I could feel the pain in these women's eyes. Pain that they had felt one way or the other and I knew instantly that I wanted to be part of the group.

Doris was a forty eight year old woman who wanted to break free from her marriage. She had no children because her husband did not want any and insisted they used protection whenever they made love to each other. Doris was a quiet woman and she said very little. She loved kids and had always wanted to hold her children in her hands but was left conflicted when her husband made it known to her that he did not want kids.

"I do not think men are bad people in general," she said to me when I told her I hated all men. "People, in general, are either good or bad. There are good men just as much as there are good women out there; and then there are the bad men just as much as there are bad women. Some of us are just unlucky and we get to meet with the bad ones. I spoke a lot about having kids with my husband before we got married and I had told him I would love to have two baby girls and I was going to call them Lara and Laura. He joked about it and said that he would have preferred boys and I told him it did not matter, that I would love them regardless. Oh my! On our honeymoon he insisted we used protection because he did not want us to make a mistake." There was so much pain in her eyes and she had let a little tear slip from the corner of her eyes. She felt so lost and betrayed.

"Do not think you are the only one who has a husband who does not respect his wife. He beats me! He does not want children and yet he beats me! I am so glad that you have found this group at a very young age because I wish I did! Cheryl has made me stronger and better than I was before I met her and I know that you will be too."
"Do you want to leave him?" I asked her.
"Oh yes! Every one of us wants to. I am working on it and getting divorced would be the best gift I would ever have and I would love to give myself that when I turn fifty."

Doris was a nice woman who loved kids and I could not imagine the pain she felt when she did not have children. Her eyes sparkled with joy each time she played with my boys.

"Even if it is just one kid, I do not mind. I just want to have mine. Is that too much to ask?" Alison was a beautiful forty-one-year-old woman. She got married when she was thirty-five. Her husband was thirty-five too. He was nothing she had imagined him to be. She had met him when she was twenty-six years old and they had been friends for a long time. They had dated for a few months before they tied the knot. He eventually fell in love with a model and they got divorced. He got married to his model girlfriend just weeks after they had divorced. Alison was yet to recover from the shock when I joined the group. She had two children for him but he had gained custody of the children.

"What can I do? He has the money and influence and I have nothing. No court would want to give the children to a pauper."

Cheryl had been on her case for years. She had friends who had taken up Alison's case but it was yet to advance to something good. Barbara was a medical doctor that was married to a deadbeat dad. He was a drug addict who would not get his act together. She had known him since they were in high school and she had gone to college while he dropped out.

"I cannot believe I allowed myself to get knocked up by Jimmy!"
"I guess the sex really messes you up, you are not thinking straight."
"I guess so! He does not care about the kids and he is terrible with money. He collects money from me every time and if I do not give him, he beats me up!" She said as she burst into tears.

Carol was a few years older than me and her husband left her when she had a fire accident and her face and body got burned.
"It was never about love. I guess he married me for my beauty and when I lost it, he left me." I had seen Carol's pictures before the accident and she was stunning. It is so sad that we live in a world where people are superficial and they marry for looks. Melissa was fifty when she chose to walk away from her marriage. "It was a hard decision to make, but I just had to leave. He cheated on me constantly and I could not take it anymore!"

We were women who were hurt and broken. Our husbands chose not to honor the bedrock of our marriage and we had to unite to pull each other up. I am grateful that these women are a part of my success story.

CHAPTER 3

"I can do all things through Christ that strengthens me." Phil 4:13.

Babies are cute and are a gift from God. This verse in the Bible was a game-changer for me. My first son was a handful and when I gave birth to him, I cried. I did not cry because I didn't want him. I cried because I was glad I had given birth to him safely. The nine months that I carried him were the toughest months of my life. I had God and my mother who continued to pray for me over the phone. Who said motherhood is easy? Well, it was not an easy journey for me but I am thankful I was able to scale through the hurdles of being a mother.

Motherhood

Parenting is not an easy task and it is even more daunting when you have to do it alone. I took care of our first son all by myself and my ex-husband was rarely ever at home. He brought the money to take care of the home and all that, but I believe that there is more to being a husband and a father than just bringing money home. I tell people that anybody can bring money home. Anybody can pay a child's school fees and buy the child clothes and toys. Family is more than that. Don't get me wrong and I am not saying those things are not important, but other factors make up a home.

How Motherhood Changed My Life.

There is no better way to put this, but motherhood surely changes your life. It changed mine! I was no longer the same person I was before I had kids and I had to start thinking about somebody else apart from myself. It became an entirely new world for me the minute I found out I was pregnant. I was confused and I remembered sitting across from the doctor when she broke the news to me. I am not ashamed to say that I never knew that I was pregnant before I visited the doctor. I was sick and I went to the hospital. I wouldn't say the signs were not there, but they were not as visible as I thought they were going to be. I was pregnant for six months and I didn't know. It's kind of mind-boggling, right? How dare a woman say she didn't know she had a baby inside her? Oh! She must be a bad and nonchalant woman to not have noticed that she had a growing human inside of her. However, things are not always black and white and there is that grey area where things just happen and disregard nature! Maybe I was just not in tune with my body. Maybe I was nonchalant! Or just maybe I was pregnant and just did not know! It happens and there are many women out there who never knew they were pregnant until it was time to deliver the baby!

Signs I Think I Ignored.
- **I Was Always Tired.**

To be fair, I was always tired even before I got pregnant. I think that was one of the reasons why I did not know at the time that I was pregnant. Before the pregnancy, I was physically and mentally drained. I did not have a job and I was a stay-at-home wife. I cooked and cleaned and I had gotten so used to it that it was no longer a problem for me. However, there was one issue, the unending cleaning and arguments in the home. Unending cleaning meant that there was hardly any time I had to rest simply because my ex-husband was not a neat person. Either he was not a neat person or he was a neat person and he chose to be inconsiderate. It was annoying because we were two adults who lived together but the other refused to get his act together. He would mess up the toilet I had just cleaned and I would have to clean it all over again. He left his clothes everywhere in the house and in short, he was a mess. So I cleaned and cleaned all the time.

He did not like to see his house dirty and he complained whenever there was a bit of dirt somewhere. What bothered me the most was the fact that he wanted a clean house yet he refused to be clean. I was working to get the house clean and he was working against me. **Bonus tips for women; marry someone who will work with you with love and not someone who wants to bring you down.**

When we get pregnant, our progesterone increases and we become tired, weak and drained. I felt that, but I never thought It had anything to do with me being pregnant. I got married at the age of nineteen. I do think that was one of the reasons why I didn't know I was pregnant. I might be wrong but I think it affected me strongly. I didn't know much about my body.

- **I Lost Weight.**

Sounds funny, but it's true. I lost weight when I was pregnant with my first son. It was not a surprise for me that I was losing weight faster than I could imagine. I was not happy in my marriage, I worried a lot, I was always working and my ex-husband did hit me a couple of times. So I was losing weight and had attributed it to my sufferings.

- **I Did Not Want to Eat.**

I love food! While I was pregnant with my first son, I did not want to eat. I was unhappy and angry, eating became a chore. Or so I thought. Foods I loved to eat became the enemy. They smelled weird and always made me feel nauseous. At first, I thought I was mad at myself and it was getting in the way of my appetite.

Motherhood is a beautiful thing when you choose to embrace it. I know there are women out there who dread motherhood and do not want to ever have kids. Yes, it happens in life. Not everyone wants to have children and that is okay. However, if you are reading this book and you hope to be a mother someday, then you will have to learn how to embrace motherhood. It didn't matter that I did not have the family I always wanted, because the minute I touched my son's hands and I saw his face, I knew that I had birthed the most beautiful boy in the world.

Bear in mind that you would have to cater for another life. You are responsible for bringing the child into this world and now that the baby is here, you simply have to nurture the baby. From there on you know that you have mouths to feed, clothes to wash and diapers to change. Be prepared to watch the baby grow, laugh and make mistakes. Motherhood changes people and so many things will change when you become a mother. Your relationships will change, friendships will change and even your daily routines will change.

The Support System
The first thing I think of when it comes to a support system is family. There is nothing like having your family solely behind you and you know that if anything happens, you have people who have your back. I believe every human should have a strong support system, regardless of how much you think you can do it alone. A support system comprises people who are around you, love you and care for you. They encourage you and see to it that you are making the best decisions. They know that it is not an easy thing to be a mother and they understand the many struggles. They do not make you feel

badly when you make mistakes, because you are human and you do not know it all. These types of systems exist and sadly some women do not have them. Your support system could be your husband, children (if this is not your first time), mother, father, friends, church brethren (if you attend one), colleagues, etc. I highly encourage new mothers to have a support system. In my case, I had my mother. She was there for me when I felt my world crumbling. She was my support and pillar. I do not know what I would have become if she was not there for me.

What Happens When Your Support System Does Not Want to be Supportive?
Some support systems do not want to be supportive and you would have to come to terms with that fact. In my case, my mom was there for me, but my ex-husband was not. I remember when my water[1] broke and I was so scared I thought I was going to die or lose the baby. I called my ex-husband but he told me to call my mom! I guess I should have called my mom first and not bother him. Life is not perfect and sometimes things do not go the way you planned them. I called my mom and she came running down to meet me at the hospital.

Sometimes, the people around you might not be supportive and you are all alone. It is okay because these things happen a lot and you are not the first person. I will not say that I got through motherhood alone because I had my mother. Sadly, I did feel alone a lot. My mom had a job and life of her own, so at some points, I was alone. It irks me when men try to shift the responsibility of taking care of the children, unto purely financial provision and some men do not even provide any financial help at all. In their defense, they would say that they have provided money and material things for the family, what

---
1. The amniotic fluid that the baby swims around in is released from the uterus as a sign that the body is preparing to birth the baby.

more? Fast forward, today the world has changed drastically. Women now work and make money just as much as men and some women even make more money than their husbands.

Many people told me that I had no right to complain because my husband was the provider of the household. I did not have to open my mouth to say a word and I had to be submissive. Do all the house chores, give birth and shut up. A man getting out of the house to provide for the family is fine, but it only becomes a problem if the woman wants to pursue her dreams too. Dreams and aspirations are not pertinent to a particular gender!

Motherhood and Professional life
Motherhood does not come with a manual. So many women learn on the job and from the experiences of others. Many women know men who are caring and supportive of their dreams. These men understand where they are coming from and where they are going in life. While other women do not have these types of men in their lives, it bothers me to see women like this in need of help. I was one of those women and I know how it felt to be alive and yet shrink as time passes. Is motherhood a bad thing? No! Motherhood is and should be a beautiful thing for every woman. Motherhood should be celebrated! Some women choose motherhood and do not care about what happens outside of motherhood. Other women choose motherhood and still care about what happens outside motherhood. They do not view motherhood as something that should absorb their entire lives. They have dreams and aspirations and do not think that their lives should be put on permanent hold.

Being a mom shouldn't stop you from being a doctor, nurse, teacher, writer, therapist, hair stylist, or any other profession; or prevent you from pursuing any other passion or dream. Women support their husband's dreams even when it's not convenient, so why should men not do the same? Most men tend to bring up the term submission but do they know what the term submission means? Ironically, they forget the scripture which says that husbands should love their wives as Christ loved the Church and laid down His life for her. Christ died for the Church but so many men are out there speaking about submission with no intention of showing love to their wives. Submission is an act of will based on trust and respect gained for the significant other.

Motherhood is a demanding job, so there is little wonder that some women are okay with just being stay-at-home mothers. Motherhood is a job that begins immediately when you find out you are pregnant. Your pregnancy is your appointment letter. Then you invest your time and energy in nurturing your body because whatever you do at that moment, affects the baby in the womb. At this point, some women give up their dreams to start nurturing the unborn baby as they prepare themselves for motherhood, while some other women do not think it is necessary. It does not matter what these women pick, the most important thing is they are not being forced against their will or conscience. **The key is striking a balance between work and home.** This applies to both men and women. Husbands shouldn't work to the detriment of their families [I know most families can't afford that but if you can, avoid it]. There should be a time for work and a time for family. Couples should work together to find creative ways of supplementing the family income without neglecting family time.

Manage stress - Motherhood can be pretty stressful and it can be more stressful when you have to work too. Take time to relax! Give yourself breaks from work, daily house chores, etc. Go out with the girls or have a nice day out with hubby.

Eat well - Mothers make sure that everyone eats well and they shouldn't forget to eat well too. Skipping meals will drain your energy and you will not be able to function properly.

Plan your time! - Have a book where you write down all the tasks you wish to accomplish each day. Remember you do not have to have a list of many tasks that you cannot achieve. Take it slow and only jot down a few tasks. Do not beat yourself up if you do not accomplish all the tasks. You are only human!

Make time to meditate - Do not underestimate the power of meditation. Take a few minutes to do deep breathing to take you through hectic days. Meditation has been proven to do wonderful things and it helped me overcome so many challenges while I was still married.

Women in The Workplace
Women face a lot of challenges in the workplace because of a lack of support from various arenas. Not many women want to talk about it because when they do, it often comes out as if they are nagging. Many women are still expected to work full time and still come home to raise children, cook, clean and carry out other domestic chores. This is not right because we have two parents now working full time in their various professions, but one parent has to come back home to take up another job. That is not right! Before they get married, couples should determine their roles, in respect to the division of domestic duties and they should seek to arrive at a mutually agreeable arrangement that is open to adjustment as life demands.

There are some challenges women face in the workplace. These issues are not usually well addressed and when women complain, their complaints are not taken seriously and they are viewed as troublemakers. Issues like security, sexual harassment and maternity leave. These problems are not fully addressed in workplaces and when women bring them up, they are ignored. Women need to voice their opinions and come to a mutual agreement with their partners as the outcome can affect the family and the society by extension when all is said and done.

CHAPTER 4

The Status and Stigma of Marriage - The stigma that follows unmarried women cannot be overlooked. God forbid that a thirty-year-old woman is unmarried! As time passes, times are changing and more and more women are beginning to change the status quo. Back in the days where there was no supportive environment for girls concerning empowerment, development and education, marriage was the answer to everything for a female child. The girl child had nothing but the household in which she would find herself, so girls were married off as early as fifteen. Back then professional success and contribution to society as a whole did not matter. If she was not married and did not have kids, she would be deemed irresponsible and irrelevant.

Nowadays, women can provide for and take care of themselves, so they do not have to worry about who cares or does not care about them. The fact is that it is difficult for society to accept that women now are not the same as women ages ago. We have grown greatly and the world is not ready yet for fully independent women. With age, women gain experience and knowledge, but the world still views women as young, naïve and dependent (needing a man no matter what). A woman's age is viewed as a ticking time bomb. Everywhere she goes, society tells her to be quick to get married. Society reminds her that she is getting old and she needs a man! They tell her that if she does not have a man as she ages, she might never find a man. This is a sad commentary on society after all this time.

What if the Marriage is Abusive?

A good wife shuts up even in an abusive marriage. No way, this is a lie! An abusive marriage is hell and I do not wish that upon anyone. That feeling of fear that burns inside a person in an abusive marriage is a horrible experience! It is possible to be in an abusive relationship or marriage and be ignorant about it. An abusive marriage comes in different forms.

Verbal Abuse

Verbal abuse is a gateway that usually leads to other forms of abuse. This happens when the other party constantly shouts, degrades, curses and belittles you. Verbal abuse is a kind of abuse that causes emotional pain to the victim. Verbal abuse can be tricky to spot in a relationship so here are some attributes of verbal abuse:- Name-calling, threats, gaslighting[2], insults and unnecessary and constant corrections. Verbal abuse can lead to anxiety, mood swings, chronic stress, depression, decreased self-esteem, hopelessness, shame, guilt and Post Traumatic Syndrome Disorder, some times even suicide.

Emotional Abuse

This refers to psychological abuse that can also be verbal. It includes threats, curses, etc.
- Excessive texting.
- Dominating behavior.
- Controlling behavior
- Threatening behavior.
- Stalking.

---

2. Causing someone to question their own worth

- Humiliating behavior.
- Ignoring.
- Lying.
- Withholding crucial information.

It is impossible to list all the types of emotional abuse that exists because there are many. A relationship consisting of emotional abuse and devoid of physical abuse is still unhealthy. A healthy relationship shouldn't have any form of abuse whatsoever. As a person, you should learn to detect any slight form of abuse early in your relationship. Emotional abuse might not cause physical damage but it can mess with the mind and cause emotional damage.

Emotional abuse can happen to anyone and it is not subject to marriage alone. Children, teenagers and adults all experience emotional abuse. Emotional abuse does not cause physical harm but it tends to diminish people's sense of identity and can make them feel worthless in the long run. Emotional abuse follows a pattern. One party sees the other as a weaker person and proceeds to exert dominance. The abuser does not care about the other party and only feels guilty when their actions bear consequences. Then they feel sorry for a while and repeat the same actions over and over again. Emotional abuse is not always targeted at a weaker person because anybody can experience it. Sometimes, the person with lesser power in a relationship is the abuser. Excessive control or violence is then used to make up for this lack of power. If you are experiencing emotional abuse in a relationship, chances are, you are not weak but strong and your partner is just trying to bring you down. Women are not the only ones abused, men are abused too.

You should be able to spot when someone is manipulative. Manipulative people do not care about others but only themselves.

They try to force their beliefs and opinions on others and they make the other party feel guilty if they do not adopt their beliefs and opinions. They do not care what you have to say because they believe your opinion and beliefs do not matter. You are an amazing person and you should never have to put up with somebody belittling you and making you feel like a nobody! Yelling and raising your voice in a relationship is not necessarily abuse. Some people tend to lose control when they are angry and yell at the top of their voices; but how much is too much? You should learn to discern when a particular trait such as yelling shifts towards abuse.

A characteristic of abusers is that they know when to act right. The moment you realize that they are not good enough for you and you are prepared to walk away, they suddenly become nice! They become apologetic and flattering saying the nicest things you would want to hear. Such a partner makes promises to you and tells you they will change. They also make it a point of duty to let you know that nobody would want you other than them. Lies! People like that do not change! You deserve better, instead of waiting for them to change, you make the change, move on.

Physical Abuse
Physical abuse occurs when physical harm is unleashed upon the victim. I was also a victim of this type of abuse. I remember when my first son turned one and I was excited. I had succeeded in raising my baby boy to one year old. It was a big win for me. I wanted to have a party for my son to mark his first birthday because he deserved it. My ex-husband agreed with the birthday party and planning commenced. I was excited about the party and I had invited my girls over.

Maybe it was the fact that I had managed to have a few friends outside of the marriage or the fact that I had not told him I was inviting people to my son's party, but he beat me that night after William's birthday party.

He kept yelling, "How can you do this to me!"
I still do not know why I deserved the beating that night. The party was successful and William had so much fun. I caught my ex-husband throwing glances at my friends at the party with angry eyes. I could tell he was not pleased that I had friends and had invited them over to celebrate with me.

This is what happens with abusers, they always look for an excuse to hit you even when you have not done anything wrong. Abusers always feel the need to exercise their authority on others either through words or physical abuse. The first time my ex-husband hit me was three days after we got married. He came back home one afternoon while I had fallen asleep. He had knocked for hours and I was fast asleep. I did not hear him. I eventually woke up and opened the door and he punched me in my stomach immediately. I thought I was going to throw up my intestines. There was so much blood spurting out of my mouth and I could not breathe well. My breaths came in gasps and he stood there, right in front of me yelling at me. I knew at that moment that I was in trouble. He called one of his friends who was a medical doctor to come and check up on me when I kept on vomiting blood and he got scared that I was going to die.

Unfortunately, the physical abuse did not end there. I got slapped, kicked and pushed many times. I got my hair snatched and pulled all over and he would spit on me and say derogatory things to me. Getting beaten was no longer something new and I got so used to it, that I expected it to happen. My body has scars and I was ashamed to look at my body back then, but not anymore. They remind me of where I am coming from and where I am going.

Is Marriage Worth It Anymore?

As time passes by, people grow and develop and this causes culture to change with each generation. Culture encompasses the systems in which a group of people does things and this system changes with time. Generations ago, marriage was the bedrock of society. The family was the first governed institution that children were exposed to and this laid the foundation of how these children developed later in life. Marriage was the system that provided a safe environment for the prolongation of species, protection of property rights and bloodlines. So many years ago, women were acquired as property and men were allowed to become the husbands of their deceased brother's widow. Most marriages were done as an alliance between two families and rarely did people marry for love. Married people ostensibly grew to love each other as respect and companionship increased. The reasons for marriage has changed drastically over the years.

We cannot ignore the drastic evolutionary path of the institution of marriage. We see increasingly women having a choice to get married as opposed to past generations where women had no choice but to get married. Women were not allowed to work, not granted access to education, nor allowed to own land. These made it quite easy for men to become the providers and so women stayed back to take care of the home. In today's world, more women are getting educated, working, owning land and acquiring property. Women can now become providers and marriage is no longer necessary for women economically. So what then is the reason for marriage today?

I have met many women who were stuck in a marriage that brought them nothing but pain and misery and they could not walk out of the marriage because they had nothing to fall back onto. It was a case of 'He provides and if I leave, how do I care for my children?' I was one of those women. I wanted to leave countless times but I was scared that if I left, I would have nothing to fall back onto. I did not have an education or a job, how was I supposed to raise my two boys all by myself? How was I supposed to feed and protect them? These questions ran through my mind and I was in a dilemma.

I met a woman who had lost a baby because her husband hit her so badly in the belly, she lost consciousness. I was cold and angry when she narrated the story to me. I was angry with the husband for doing such a cruel thing to another person and I was also furious with her. "Leave! Take your bags and leave! Get out of there!" I told her.

"But I cannot!" She said.

"Why not?" I asked.

"I am lost, I am so lost that if I go out wandering into the world all by myself, I do not know what will happen to me or my daughter."

"You will have to leave at some point. Do it for your daughter."

I realized that I was lost too and I would not have gotten the courage to run away with my boys if I did not have Cheryl and the other girls as my support system. I felt so sorry for her, I had to tell Cheryl about her and she was invited to our support group. It is with joy that as I write this book, she has remarried and she has two more children for her present husband.

Marriage is a beautiful thing and whoever wants to get married should do so for the right reason. Nobody can determine what the appropriate age or reason for marriage should be for another person. It all boils down to you. Evaluate yourself and ask yourself questions to know if truly you understand what this institution called marriage is all about. Are you getting married for companionship? Are you getting married because you want to build a life with somebody? Are you getting married because you want to create a safe environment for your children? Are you getting married because you think your partner is your poverty alleviation scheme? Are you getting married for sex?

What Does The Bible Say About Marriage?
There is a saying that love is like a flame that burns brightly as long as it is fed. Love can be Eros, which means a sensual love that gratifies the senses. It could be Phileos, which is the love for intimacy and sharing. This includes our cherished feelings for friends and neighbors. The source of our love should come from God, it is called Agape. When your love originates from God then you will know how to love and nurture your marriage.

The Bible described marriage as a physical representation of the spiritual relationship of the body of Christ to Jesus Christ the Bridegroom. Biblically, the husband of the household is likened to Christ who is the head of the Church. Many people forget the remaining part of the scriptures that outline that husbands should love their wives even as Christ so loved the Church that He gave Himself for it. The Bible preaches that the entire ethos of the Church is based on Agape love. This type of love is sacrificial and unconditional and such love should exist in the household. Agape love is the love that glues a family together and without it, such a family can crumble. With agape love comes service, respect and forgiveness. Romantic love, Eros and Agape love are important in marriages, these two are not mutually exclusive. They work together to form the bedrock of a family. Romantic love wanes as the relationship matures but agape love is what keeps the family together through all seasons. Agape love is what makes couples love one another, respect one another and serve one another. As couples and as a family, you should love as Jesus loves. This is so vital that I would suggest that you pray for

Agape love to be developed in your heart; we all need more of it. Agape love has nothing to do with self-gratification, beauty, intimacy, or shared interests. What happens when Agape love is non-existent in a marriage and beauty and virility goes? Will there still be a marriage? What happens when the children have grown up and left the home and you are left alone with your partner, will there still be a marriage? Agape love is the love that sustains a marriage no matter what happens to a spouse's beauty, health, or finances.

Roles in Marriage
The roles in marriage have blurred over the years and they are not as clearly defined as they were typically defined years ago. The traditional role of the husband was to provide for and protect and the traditional role of the wife was to help her husband, nurture the children and run the home. This clear distinction in gender roles has been practiced for so many years and it looks as though it no longer applies in today's narrative of what gender roles are all about. More and more women are getting educated and having well-paid jobs. Women have joined in the sole duty of men to be providers and now we have families running on the system of both parents being providers. It is not a bad thing because marriage should be about multiplicity in all ramifications, but it can become a problem.

There is a category of men today who want a traditional wife and a modern wife. A traditional wife stays back at home to cook, clean and take care of the kids. A modern wife has a job and a career that brings in money to the family. These types of men want the best of both worlds but refuse to become the best of both worlds to their wives. These men cannot take up the burden of being the sole providers and they want someone to help ease their burdens but they are not ready to help their spouses ease theirs. They want a wife who has a 9-5 job just like them. She is bringing in money as well but she is also required to come back home to be a traditional wife. Women need to guard against these double standard men and make sure in the dating stage to work through all these issues.

When agape love exists in a family, it does not matter if something is considered a man's role or a woman's role. You help each other in love. Agape love makes you want to do things for your partner because you love and respect them.

The head of the family does not mean that your words are 'yea and amen.' Foolishness! Leadership is not about a specific gender. The CEO is not automatically the wisest person in the room. The head of the department is not automatically the wisest in the room. The vice president or president is not automatically the wisest in the country. The head of the family is not automatically the wisest in the family. You still need the opinions of others and you have to acknowledge the fact that as the head of the family, you can make mistakes too and that's okay. Ultimately leadership is about bringing out the best in the people around you and making the best decision for the greater good.

CHAPTER 5

Raising Children

Children are a gift from God! And it is our duty as parents to nurture them and watch them grow into beautiful and well-mannered adults in the future. Parents are not the only ones that raise children. Society and community also play a huge role in molding children. I think I am a good mom and I know that I poured my heart into my children's lives. I inculcated values into their lives and I believed I was doing a good job. It was a Thursday night in the year 2000 and I could not sleep; I tossed and turned on the bed and I was uneasy. I was divorced for ten years and I lived alone in a small apartment with my boys. William was nineteen and Robert was seventeen. It was just my teenage boys and me.

I was not exhausted that night. My body was physically fit, but my mind was not. I got down on my knees and prayed to God. "God, why? Why can't I sleep? Why this sudden unrest in my mind and heart? God, why?" I prayed and cried that night because I knew that God wanted to reveal something to me. I went to bed that night and slept like a baby. I woke up at 2 a.m. It was sudden and I knew right at that moment that my boy was in trouble. I rose from the bed and walked to my sons' room. Robert was in bed sleeping while William's bed was empty.

Fear gripped me. I remember standing in the middle of the room and my boy William was not there. I turned on the light and Robert turned on his bed and said, "Please turn off the light, mom." I was trembling and cold. The weather was good that morning, but I felt cold and confused. I knocked on the bathroom door and nobody answered, then I opened it and walked into the bathroom. I remember screaming and Robert came running towards me shouting at the top of his voice, "Mom, what is wrong!?" William was on the floor and he was dying. He had taken an overdose of cocaine and he was dying. "Call 911! Call 911, Robert!"

That very day was dark. I questioned myself and my parenthood. Was I a failed parent? Did William behave that way because his father left? Was choosing this single parenthood a mistake? Was I doomed to fail from the beginning? I felt fear in my heart that I was going to lose my son and it did not matter that I knew in my heart that I raised a good boy; he was dying as I was praying. "Lord! Have mercy on him, do not let him go!"

Sometimes as parents, we raise good children and yet the unexpected happens. The world also trains children. Parents should be careful because you can lose your children to the world. I was confused, I knew I did not raise my boy to take drugs or smoke or do anything like that, but he did. I kept asking myself where did I go wrong and where did that come from?

The World Raises Children Too.
Society plays a significant role in influencing child development. Culture and society influence your child's identity and it could be positive or negative. Children are still growing and they are not fully developed yet, so they pick both good and bad things from the people around them. They learn to speak, behave, laugh and

eat from the environment surrounding them. I did not know that William had become friends with some other children in school, that taught him that taking drugs was cool. I prayed to God and He made me correct that lie and stop that attitude before it escalated. Had I not prayed that night, I would not have known that He was walking a path of no return.

The environment is an integral part of a child's growth and development. Raising a child in an unfriendly environment could hurt the child. Most children brought up in such an environment rarely ever come out of it. Imagine having a father as a drunk? A mother as a drug addict and an uncle as a drunk too? What impact would that have on the child? Most times, children born in unsafe environments inherit such character traits and spread them to others around them. William did not have a mother as a drunk or a father as a drunk, but he fell into the wrong kind of friends.

I have often considered that he could have been more aware and understood more than I thought of the abuse I suffered from his father. Very often boys experience deep pain at being helpless to protect their mothers from abuse. He could have found drugs attractive as a way to medicate his deeply hidden pain. Sometimes, we as parents should learn to protect our children from the monsters in the world. The world is not safe for adults. Hence, it is even more unsafe for children. Children are individuals. They start their lives as totally dependent on their primary caregivers, which is the family. The healthy development of children is significant to how society develops in the future. Consequently, if the family fails, they create adults with bad attitudes who mess up society.

My Struggle as a Mother.
I became a mother at the age of twenty-one. William was the reason

why I smiled and my eyes sparkled for the first time in my marriage. I held my baby boy in my arms, I knew I had found love after seeing him for the first time. I made a promise that I was always going to be there for him. My mom was with me and she had suggested I name him William after her father. "He will make a fine young man," She had told me. The hospital had informed my ex-husband that I had just given birth and he did not come to the hospital to see me. I did not expect him to come to see us at the hospital but I was devastated when he said over the phone that he did not need to be there. The doctor told him again that I had just given birth and he repeated the answer he gave before. My mom could not come to live with us because my ex-husband had said that it was not necessary. I had to figure everything out all by myself. The year 1997 was a difficult one for me.

When I gave birth to Robert, I had pretty much figured out most of it; but it was not an easy ride because each pregnancy is different. I felt so much pain with his birth and I had gained so much weight. My ex-husband reminded me every single time. "You are ugly and fat!" It was a difficult period for me physically and mentally. My ex-husband had gained tremendous weight during our marriage, but yet he felt it was his right to remind me that I had put on so much weight because I gave birth.

The Insecurities
I looked forward to my wedding night because I had been told by so many other women that it was a special night between my husband and I. I had never had sex with a boy because I wanted to wait until I got married. I was scared and I had a lot of things going on in my head. How will it be? Will it hurt? My ex-husband had slept with so many women and he took pride in telling me each time we had sex. On the first night, he said things like, "Why are you stiff? I had a

girl who did that or did this while we slept together, so why are you stiff?" He compared me to all the girls he ever dated or had a one-night stand with. He would say that I was too short compared to the girls he had dated, or I was too fat or not as pretty as the other girls. When I first lost weight when I was pregnant with William, my ex-husband had praised me and said that I looked so much better now. He said that if I were skinnier when we got married, he would have loved me more. Losing weight did not make him love me more. He was still as evil as he was. I did not like myself in the mirror. My friends in my group had told me that I looked really good and that I should not listen to him.

I was twenty-five years old when I decided I needed to go back to school. I told my girls at our little secret hangout and they encouraged me to go back to pursue my dreams. I had to think of a way to tell my ex-husband because I already had two kids. William was four and Robert was two at that time. I knew that there was no way he would let me go back to school, so I had to think of a plan. He was always angry and he was not always at home. Most times, I spent the night alone with my kids. It did not bother me anymore that he was not always at home because I had my kids with me and I was always busy with them. My girls had promised me that they were going to have my kids with them each time that I was busy with school. Everything was well planned out and the only problem I had was looking for a way to tell my husband that I wanted to go back to school.

I had already applied to the previous school I wanted to attend when I was a teenager and I was waiting for their reply. The day I got accepted into college was when I summoned the courage to tell my ex-husband that I wanted to go to school. He was home throughout that Saturday and I had brainstormed what would be the best way to break the news to him.

'I'll tell him! I'll tell him!' I told myself. I sat down across from him on the couch and I had Robert in my lap.

"I want to go back to school," I said. The atmosphere in the room was quiet, so quiet, that I could hear my heartbeat. My ex-husband did not say anything and I knew he heard me the first time. I was scared to repeat myself. I got up from the couch and was about to leave when he pulled me by my hair. My parental instinct triggered and I held on to my boy tightly. I screamed, Robert screamed and my ex-husband kept yelling. I could feel Robert slipping from my hand and I screamed, "He will fall! He will fall!" Robert slipped from my hand and fell to the ground and I rushed to pick my baby up. At that point, William appeared at the door and he was crying. There was so much noise that day. I was crying, Robert was crying and Williams was crying.

He pulled me back and I could not hold Robert and I begged him, "I am not going anymore, let me go," but he did not listen. He pulled me and dragged me to the bathroom and immersed my face in the bathtub. I felt life draining out of my body and I thought I was going to die but the will to live and be there for my boys was very strong so I fought back. I gave him a blow in his groin with my elbow and ran out of the bathroom. I grabbed the boys, William in one hand and Robert in the other. I ran out of our apartment building and I kept running until my strength waned.

I wanted to go back home but I knew that he was going to look for us at my mother's house. In the final analysis I did not go back home. I ended up staying in a women's shelter for about three weeks.

CHAPTER 6

Financial Problems

The moment I decided to walk away from my marriage was when I started to have money problems. The kids were too young to understand that mommy did not have money anymore because she never had! She walked away from their daddy and his money. The devil has a way of doing things. He makes us doubt ourselves and I started to doubt myself, whether I could raise my boys all by myself. He made me think that I needed my ex-husband to make it in life but he was wrong! We lived in a small one-bedroom apartment very close to my college, so I did not have to worry about transportation to school. My friends from the ladies group were kind enough to pick up my children from my house because I could not go to where they lived because I could run into my ex-husband.

Single parents are at high risk of having financial problems, which can, in turn, affect their overall wellbeing. Financial problems are one thing many people do not want to talk about. It affects everybody, both the married and the unmarried. People should not shy away from having money discussions. Most single parents have financial problems because they now have to raise a family with just a single income. It becomes even more problematic if they earn meager incomes.

Keeping Food on the Table.

'I am hungry mom,' William had cried the first night we moved to our new apartment. I had run out of the money Cheryl and the other ladies had given me. I did not know what else to do and it was not fair to go back to the ladies to beg for more money. I was not prepared for my financial problems after leaving my husband. I was scared and I acted on impulse and left for my safety and that of my children. I had to think of the best way to take care of the kids considering our circumstances. William reminded me again that he was hungry...

"I will get food soon," I told him.

"But I am hungry," He insisted.

I had two boys crying in my living room and I was confused. I had spent the money I was given on rent, clothes, appliances and food. When we ran out of food, I had no money to restock. I had just five dollars in my purse and I was skeptical about spending it.

"I will get food."

And then the crying continued and I almost cried too, but I had to be brave for my boys.

I got a job in a restaurant close to my home and I earned little money. Child support was an issue because I was not legally divorced at the time I ran away from the house. My mom had to stop walking because she had developed pain in her spine, so it was difficult for her to work. I could not ask her for any money, I was all alone. Taking care of necessities such as food and clothing became a priority. I could not afford all the things the boys wanted because my ex-husband had always gotten them many toys in the past.

After working for a while at the restaurant, I was able to pay my school fees and take care of the boys. Cheryl had helped me out with my finances. Cheryl taught me how to budget as a single mom and that helped me throughout my journey of single parenthood. The restaurant was a small one and I was one of two waitresses who worked there for very long hours. I left the boys with Carol and she helped take care of the boys while I worked and studied at the same time. I made $6.5 per hour, which was barely enough to do anything. I mostly worked when I was not having classes because I needed extra hours to make ends meet. The other lady I worked with had no problems working for twenty-four hours because she was not a student and she did not have children.

Keeping food on the table was a struggle for me. I was not bothered that I had no food to eat, but I always made sure my boys ate good food. It was a struggle and I am thankful it paid off in the end. This is one of the realities of single motherhood.

Juggling Time
Time was something I did not have back then. I was a financially challenged single mother who needed more time on her hands. I needed time to work and make money and I needed time for school. Any single mother in college would understand what I am saying. I have to be there for my family, provide for them and have good grades. None was more important than the other, but at some point, I had to do more and more of some things and less of other things. The intense amount of time needed to study and attend classes clashed with the time needed to make money and vice versa. The bigger the boys grew, the more money I had to spend. I had to think of schools, clothes and they ate huge portions of food. I needed more money to keep up with my expenses.

The restaurant became more demanding when the other waitress quit her job. I became the only waitress and that meant I had to spend more time working. I would drop the boys off at school before heading to the restaurant and Carol helped me pick the kids up from school. They stayed with her until I got back from the restaurant, usually around nine p.m. I saw less and less of my kids every day and it broke my heart.

Getting the degree I always wanted became impossible because my grades were getting worse every single day. Sometimes, I skipped classes because I needed to work and other times I missed work because I needed to attend classes and study. Mr. Mike was the owner of the restaurant and he was furious whenever I missed work. Carol had suggested I speak with the manager of the restaurant to lessen the time I was spending at the restaurant. It was a good plan and we had rehearsed the things I was going to say and I was positive that I was going to convince him. Mr. Mike did not give me the chance to explain my situation before he fired me. I was devastated and I did not know what to do. I begged him to let me stay on the job, but he refused. He had gotten two other people to replace me because he felt I was incompetent.

Courting Trouble
Not having a job meant I had more time on my hands to go to school and be there with my family but that meant less money to take care of the expenses around the house. Being a single parent is a dangerous zone especially when you are financially disadvantaged. It is like walking into a minefield and if you are not careful enough, things could blow up in your face. You might want to run back to the source of your income before the breakup or divorce. There were many times I felt it was better to go back to him. I felt lost. I could not take care of my children and I thought I needed him.
This is where I suggest having a support system. There were so many times when I thought having been beaten up by my ex-husband was

the price I had to pay if I wanted to provide a good life for my kids. Thankfully, I had the girls to tell me frankly that I was not thinking right. I remember crying over the phone telling Cheryl I wanted to go back home and she called an emergency meeting with the ladies.

"You do not want to go back to him," Barbara had told me.
"You are just confused and you are letting your emotions rule your thoughts."
"Your husband does not care about you or the kids, if he did, he would not treat you or the kids the way he does. You do not need him or anyone else to take care of you or your kids, you can do that all by yourself. We know you can do this because you are a strong woman. You will find someone who would love and respect you and your kids, but that person is not your husband." Cheryl had said.

Those words stuck with me for life. "You will find someone who would love and respect you and your kids, but that person is not your husband." The ladies gave me some money when I got another job as a waitress in another restaurant a little farther away from where I lived. I had to take a twenty minute bus drive to and back from work.

CHAPTER 7

Invest in Yourself

The best gift you can ever give to yourself is to invest in yourself. I made the decision so many years ago to go back to college and it was the best decision that I ever made. When you see yourself as a priceless piece of jewelry, others will treat you like one. As a person, you do not need to seek the approval of others, rather you can invest in yourself. Remember, you owe the world your awesomeness, do not hide it. I met a nineteen-year-old lady while I was in college and we hit it off immediately. She was fun to be with and I was amazed as to how well she carried herself compared to how I was at that age. I was twenty-seven years old when we met, but I couldn't help but admire the confidence she exuded when she spoke, laughed and walked. The aura of maturity was all over her and we had so many amazing conversations.

She was shocked when I told her I was married but separated and I had two boys. "Are you sure?" She asked. I looked at her in confusion. What did she mean by "Are you sure?"

"What do you mean?" I asked her.

"I know so many girls my age or older who are single mothers studying here, but they do not always get their act together. It is usually a mess and they always drop out later on, how do you do it?" She said.

How did I do it? This is a question that people always throw at me and I am always left in confusion. The complexity of the question has always plagued my mind and whenever I tell people that I do not know, they frown at me. Why would they react like that? Is it because they think that I have this magical secret that could change the lives of single mothers forever? I remember standing in front of my friend, speechless. "How do you do it?" She asked again.

I did not give her an answer that day or any other day. Then, I wasn't aware that there was a perfect answer or secret formula that I utilized to get me to where I am today. I struggled and persisted until I no longer needed to struggle and I think that was how I was able to break free from the pain and sorrow that I had felt in my heart. I knew in my heart that I was not where I was supposed to be yet and I knew that God had a plan for my life. The urge to act on God's plan for my life drove me back to college. Looking back now, I feel that the drive to complete it once and for all, I believe, was the secret. I had a story and I was not ready to repeat that chapter in my life. I dropped out of college just before I accepted my admission and it was not an option to reject it again.

At some point in the journey, I wanted to give up. I was torn and broken. I thought I was going to fail again! Having these negative thoughts took a toll on me because I thought I was a failure. Subsequently, I began to manifest such traits in my life. It was scary. I failed so many courses in my first year in college and one of my professors had called me into her office and she had a nice conversation with me. She asked me why I kept failing and I burst into tears. It happened involuntarily and I tried to stop myself from crying, but the more I tried, the more I cried. She did not say a word. She sat across from me and watched me cry for a very long time and then she handed a tissue over to me when she saw that my tears were waning.

"Why are you crying?" She asked.

"I am tired. I thought coming back here was going to be a good thing for me but it is hard. I have two jobs and two boys and I have college. I am just one person and yet I have to do all these things to survive. I am just so tired." I answered.

"What about the father of your boys?"

"He was not much of a father when we were with him and he is not one now. He brought the money, but that was it. He was going to kill me and my boys at some point so we had to leave." I told her still sobbing.

"I am really sorry about that. You could take some time off school and come back when you are ready." She said.

"I am ready now. There are many challenges, but I am ready. If I leave now, I do not think that I will ever be ready to come back."

"Your grades are bad and if it continues like that, you might have to leave."

"I am well aware of that and I am trying."

"You are not trying enough because if you were, your grades will be going up and not the other way round." She said firmly.

Why would she say such a thing to me? I felt attacked! How dare a stranger tell me I was not trying enough! I was a full-time student who worked two jobs and had two boys and she had the guts to sit across from me and tell me to my face that I was not trying hard enough. I was furious!

"How badly do you want this?" She asked me.

"Want what?" I answered.

"College, how badly do you want college?"

"Badly." I said.

In response to me she explained, "I was a single mother who got pregnant at the age of eighteen. Eighteen was the year I thought I had found myself and I felt it was the right thing to do to move out of my parent's house. I moved in with my boyfriend who was also eighteen years old. We were in love and it seemed like it was just us against the world. I got pregnant within one year we stayed together and that was it. He was not ready to be a father and I was not ready to get rid of the baby, so he walked away. I went back to college and made my life make sense again. It is not going to be easy and crying will not help you. Go out there and make your life make sense!"

I believe that my meeting with my professor back then was divine. I was not the only one who failed many courses in my first year. I got to know that I was the only one she called to her office. Why me? I took it upon myself right at that moment to make my life make sense. Complaining and crying are normal because we are humans and we have to let out our emotions at some point. However, I had to do something to change my situation, it was not going to be easy, but I had to make it work.

How Badly Do You Want This?

Girls should start believing in themselves and they should know that they can do all things through Christ that strengthens them. You do not need anybody to tell you otherwise, because God has already said that with Him you shall do exploits. Go be the doctor, engineer, writer, dancer, baker, CEO, or anything you want in this life, because you can. Nobody has the right to tell you otherwise!

CHAPTER 8

The question you should ask yourself as a woman is, are you your types' type? Do you see yourself in your partner, or do you just have unrealistic standards?

Standards and Preferences
Know your standards and preferences and acknowledge it if you are selling yourself short or if they are unrealistic. What are your preferences? What do you like about the opposite sex? What do you expect from the opposite sex? What can you accept and reject? Do you know what you are looking for in a relationship? Or are you one to just follow the crowd?

Some women do not have standards and preferences and this has ruined many relationships. This attitude stems from a lack of confidence and they believe they are lucky to get whatever man comes their way! That is dangerous thinking! I believed that my ex-husband was the only one that could ever love me and I was wrong. I thought that I was incapable of being loved by someone else and this ruined my self-esteem.

Do you meet men that fit into the personality you are looking for in

Are You Your Types' Type?

a man? Are you meeting the right men or the wrong ones?

The most important standard starts with yourself. Before you assess your standards, work on yourself and establish these standards within yourself. If you want a God-fearing person, be a God-fearing person yourself. To help you better understand your standards and preferences, you will need to ask yourself a series of questions.

- What kind of behavior are you willing to accept from him?
- What will you reject?
- What kind of partner do you want?
- Where are you likely to meet him?
- How do you intend on meeting him?
- What are your goals and aspirations?
- Are the people around you helping you achieve such goals and aspirations?
- What do you need to do to improve your life to meet him?

There are many more questions to ask yourself because only you can determine what you want and need in a relationship. When you have the answers to these questions, it will be an eye-opener for you. Embarking on this journey could be scary at first because you have to work on yourself and change your behavior.

Everyone has standards and yet not everyone is willing to admit that they have them. One sets standards to protect themselves and ensure that their basic needs are met by others. So you should be very clear about what behaviors are acceptable from your prospective partner such as:- they should act in a loving, honest and trustworthy manner. They should have values that align with yours. Trust is something your partner should earn from you and not get given to him by you glibly. If your partner cannot behave in the basic ways you expect him to behave, then he cannot earn your trust. If he is not emotionally available, has no integrity, is unfaithful and disrespectful, he is below standard and does not deserve your trust, much less a life with you.

How to Maintain Standards

After my divorce from my ex-husband, I set up standards that I upheld religiously. These standards did not mean that I was a narcissist or a bad person. I had evaluated myself and reinstated the standards that I had before I met him and added some more. Standards are our honorable principles that we pilot our lives by, sometimes referred to as our values. These standards act like our distinctive laws that govern our intentions, choices and decisions. When we talk about standards, we have forgotten that everyone has different standards. It would be unfair to impose our standards on others and vice versa.

In establishing standards in a relationship, having compatible standards with your partner is non-negotiable. There has to be some things that align with that of your partner. Everything about you and him could be different. You might differ in height, weight, culture, ethnicity, age, interests, wealth, but if you have conflicting standards/values, it can lead to an insurmountable obstacle in the relationship. Most times, couples' compatibility matches naturally because they share the same faith or religion and come from the same town. Oftentimes, where we come from shapes our principles and philosophies which is the driving force of our standards/values. We can become naturally attracted to people who match and align with our standard.

Attracting Opposites

I call them opposites because they do not have the same standards as you. They go against everything you believe and trust. Some standards could slightly differ and could be ignored, but large discrepancies in standards are a disaster. You are not compatible and that's it.

How serious is that? It can ruin you. When you meet a man who has different standards from what you have, you begin to feel that your standards are too high and you might want to compromise. Compromising your core beliefs and values could lead to lower self-esteem and you lose your confidence. When you begin to doubt your standards and lower them, you begin to lose yourself and the relationship could suffer.

We all come from different backgrounds and we have differing views about life. If someone is truncating your standard, you will feel it. Pay attention to that feeling because you will notice that you are no longer on the right path. Your perception about yourself and the world begins to drift. There were numerous red flags out there when I was in a relationship with my ex-husband. From the first day I met him, I should have known. Sadly, the truth is, sometimes the signs are out there but we choose to ignore them because we are so fascinated with the shiny package, we fail to look past the allure and beauty of it.

Sometimes, we are our own enemies. My ex-husband and I had nothing in common when it came to our views about the world and faith. He wanted sex before marriage and I was not in support of that. It was glaring the minute he said so, that we were not compatible. I should have walked away and that would have prevented all the trauma I had to pass through. Regrettably, I stayed and tried to reason with him and he got angry! He was angry that I did not want to sleep with him before marriage and more so that I disagreed with him! He called me a virgin that was going to die old and alone! He told me that nobody will ever love me! Those words got to me. What if he was right? Fear shook me and immobilized me and I thought he was the only man that was going to love me. I wanted him badly and I did not want him to leave me.

I doubted myself and my belief and at some point, I felt it was ridiculous to hold to the notion that premarital sex was a sin. I thought I was crazy and I thought he was sane. I was nineteen and he was thirty-five years old. A great disparity in age. He was at the age where he was thriving in his life. He had the career he wanted but I on the other hand still had a lot ahead of me. When he said he was going to leave me, I panicked. What if I did not find somebody else? I made a huge mistake when I gave in to the pressure. That compromise of one of my key principles led to the downfall of the others. The sad thing about my situation was that I did not feel better about myself. I felt worse after the sex and I knew that I had betrayed myself and God. It became difficult to say no after that and I found myself compromising all of my beliefs and principles until I had none left. He told me I was doing the right thing and I did not have to worry because he loved me so much, he was never going to hurt me. That was a complete lie!

Create Your Standard
You must create a working standard for yourself. With that, you will have a clear idea as to what you should expect in a relationship. Have a list of what you want in a man in your head or write it down on paper. You do not have to follow it verbatim, but it will act as a blueprint for you. The blueprint can contain things like personality, educational background, job, appearance, intelligence, compatibility and what the future looks like. It will help you to know if your current relationship is on track with the things you want in life.
If you are a career-oriented person and you meet someone who is a 'hippie', it can pose a problem for your relationship if he does not

meet your standards. If smoking is a deal-breaker for you and he smokes and you like everything about him except that he smokes, it can cause challenges.

Beware of Hypocrites
It sounds funny but hypocrites do not only exist in everyday life but also in churches. Learn to spot hypocrites long before entering into a relationship and stay away from them. Hypocrites are people who pretend to have beliefs, feelings, opinions, virtues and qualities. Hypocrisy can also be seen as double standards. Hypocrisy comes in many forms, some include;
- Lies and excuses.
- Saying one thing and doing another.
- Having one standard for you and they behave the opposite

He might present himself in a certain way making you think that both of you are compatible. He might believe in premarital sex and claim that he does not. Then you become invested in the relationship, only to find out later on that he was just pretending. You start the relationship on the basis that you will not have premarital sex and as the relationship advances, he begins to pester you for sex and he tries to talk you out of waiting. This happens a lot and it is a tactic used to lure women into lowering their standards. Some women fall into this trap because they are already emotionally invested in the relationship, it might become difficult to say no.

A hypocritical relationship is based on lies and deceit. One of my friends back in college was in a relationship like that and it took her a very long time to realize that her whole relationship had been built on a lie. She had told him she was not in support of premarital sex earlier in the relationship and he agreed. He had told her that he was a principled person who valued the institution of marriage and was working towards it. My friend was happy and she thought she had gotten the relationship she finally deserved. She did not know that he was cheating on her with other ladies and she only got to know two years into the relationship. He lied about his values only to get her to be in a relationship with him while he was having affairs. When she confronted him, he blamed it on her and said that she was the one who caused it because of her belief about no sex before marriage. He had been sexually active since he was fifteen and that there was no way he was going to become celibate for her. She was shattered and broken. He gave her an ultimatum to either sleep with him or walk away.

She was in love with him and she would have compromised her standards, had I not told her to walk away. This is what I call hypocrisy as many were pastors or even deacons in the Church but they appeared to prey on these women who seem to be quiet and godly and are labelled a 'Church girl' because they stick to their spiritual values. Many of these hypocrites think that these girls can be easily deceived so they pose as so-called, 'men of God' and they preach one thing but their actions reveal the opposite and they turn out to be predators.

Two-Faced People
Paul said in the Bible that, "Love should be without hypocrisy." It should not be two-faced. A two-faced person is a dangerous person and such a person can ruin your life. They have a personality they display to the public and the one they unleash in private. I am talking about a pastor that preaches love on the pulpit and beats his wife in secret. I am talking about a person who acts like a well-mannered person initially and the minute you get comfortable with them, they display their true intentions. There are so many people out there who are two-faced beings. Their public face is not in alignment

with their private face. My ex-husband was a two-faced person who harbored so much hypocrisy in him. The only people who knew him for who he truly was, were just me and my boys. I remember when his mom visited. The atmosphere in the house changed completely. He became so nice to me that he had helped me out in the kitchen while his mom watched in joy.

"This is beautiful," she said. "You are a happy family." I wished his mom came often because she brought out a false sweetness in him. A type of sweetness that screamed pretense. I knew it was all a farce. The way he looked me in the eye seductively while she watched us and the way he stared at me with those angry dark eyes the minute she looked away. He laughed too hard when she was around and he torched me often. He played with my hair, touched my neck, hand and waist. When he picked up the boys to play with them they were scared. They were so little back then, but they knew that he was dangerous. So they cried and his mom hurried to take them from him and they stopped crying. He had looked at me in anger and his eyes screamed, "How dare they embarrass me in front of my mom!" I knew at that moment that I and my boys were going to be beaten so badly immediately after she left the house. I was right!

It can be difficult to spot a two-faced person. This means that you have to pay close attention to what they say, what they do and how they do it. Watch and pray! Pray that God exposes anything they could be concealing from you and then open your eyes. Do not let your love or infatuation cloud your judgment. No matter how much you love them, try as much as possible to be realistic in every situation you find yourself in.

Narcissists
Narcissists have an inflated ego and an over vaulting sense of their

importance. They think that they are above others and superior to the point where they have no regard for anyone else. A narcissist will make a bad future partner. How do you stop yourself from being a narcissist or falling in love with a narcissist? There is also a need to be able to differentiate between a narcissist and someone who is overconfident. It can be said that narcissism usually develops from childhood. It could stem from parents who often build-up their children's confidence. It is logical and natural for parents to want their children to do well and be great. On balance it is good for children to believe in themselves and aspire to achieve greater things than their parents. However, when parents teach their children to believe that they are better than themselves and the rest of the world; this is dangerous as the children overestimate their abilities. Narcissism could also stem from a parent's neglect, where a child was not given due physical and emotional support.

Narcissists have inflated egos and are usually self-deluded and this behavior comes from a place of hurt and low self-esteem. Any slight criticism to a narcissist can lead to great hurt thereby triggering their narcissistic defence mechanism which is often anger and outbursts. Some narcissists tend to be overly confident and less sensitive. They take pride in talking about themselves a lot and they do not care about others. For example, a narcissist might decide to walk away from a relationship because they feel that they are not getting the special treatment they think they are entitled to. They have a really difficult time loving someone else because they have not truly learned how to love themselves.

It is very easy to become drawn to a narcissist because of how big they portray their personalities and then it makes you feel as if you must be as great since they have chosen you.

How Do You Know Your Partner Is A Narcissist?

- **Everything is all about them:** If you meet a man who does not care to know about you and only cares about himself, run! When having conversations with a man, pay attention to what he says and his body language. If he is all about himself and redirects every conversation to himself, he might be a narcissist. Narcissists crave attention and they think that they are better than others. They want every decision, thought, opinion, goal and choice to be all about them. They believe the world revolves around them.
- **Narcissists do not know when to stop:** They cannot detect the boundaries others have set or they can but choose to ignore it.
- **They want you all to themselves:** They isolate you and cut you off from friends and family. They try to gain control over your finances, hobbies and workforce.
- **They disregard your feelings:** Everything is all about them, so why should they care about you? They speak in absolutes and use very tactless and hurtful terms.
- **They are manipulative:** Most people can detect when someone is trying to be manipulative, but narcissists have a sneaky way of manipulating others. They belittle you at any opportunity they get and it can be in public or in private. It does not matter because all they care about is how they can have their way. They always act like the victim in every circumstance even when they are wrong. Get ready to be 'thrown under the bus' as they will not take the blame for their actions. It naturally has to be your fault no matter how far fetched it is in reality, they will make you culpable.

What Should You Do If Your Partner Is a Narcissist?

Awareness is important. Be knowledgeable about certain behaviors that people put out. Educate yourself about what the concept of narcissism is all about and understand the characteristics or the traits. If you find out that your partner exhibits all the traits of a narcissist, then you are left with the choice of sticking with your partner or walking away. Only you know your limit.

Entitlement
Entitlement comes in various ways. If you are a single mom who gets offended because others including your mother refuse to babysit for you, then you are behaving entitled. It could come in a way that one party is angry because they do certain things for their significant other and the other person does not do it for them. Some people believe they are entitled to determine how others should and should not behave. This often brings resentment and anger, forgetting that you should do things for others because you want to and not because you are expecting something in return. Entitled people believe that you owe them something even when you do not owe them anything. Entitled people believe that they are deserving of unearned privileges. Some entitlement traits include;
- Having a lack of understanding of other people's needs.
- They are narcissists because they have inflated egos and a sense of self-importance.
- Double standards. They believe that what belongs to you belongs to them also and what belongs to them, belongs to them. Such people are usually ungrateful because they do not appreciate the little things that you do for them.

Entitlement is a disease that has plagued so many relationships. My ex-husband displayed that sort of self-importance because he was the provider of the home. He felt entitled to treat me and the kids in whatever way he pleased because he paid the bills.

Most people get married with some sort of entitlement and this stems from social conditioning. We have been conditioned to believe that if the world is not black, then it is white. In some cultures, the female child is subjected to the mentality and entitlement that just because she is female she is entitled to a man's money. Also, some men have the mentality that because they are men, they can do whatever they want to a woman, just because they are men. It is this sense of entitlement that makes men become rapists and abusers. They believe that they are stronger and superior and so they can treat women in whatever way they want.

The Development of Self
As women, we should desire personal growth. Personal growth and development is a process that takes time. You just have to be consistent at it. If you feel you need to lose weight to get the body you want, go to the gym and work on your body. If you feel that you need that level of education to land your dream job, go get the degree or do that course! Examine yourself and determine what your problem areas are. Such areas could be financial, emotional, spiritual, physical and intellectual.

The Process
- Identify your current state.
- Identify your desired state.
- Determine what needs to be done to achieve the desired state.
- Set small, specific, achievable steps to get to that goal
- Find an accountability partner [friend] to help you stay on target

CHAPTER 9

When we start thinking about negative things, we begin to believe those negative things. When my ex-husband abused me for years, I started to believe those negative things that he said. It took me a while to desist from such beliefs. I met a lady in college who was in an abusive relationship with her parents and no matter what she did, it was never good enough for them. She had a grade **B** in one of our courses in her second year and when she told her parents over the phone, it was war. She was crying at the same time while she spoke on the phone and her parents kept yelling, "You are stupid for getting a **B,** what about an **A** grade?"

Be Careful What You Think!

My friend started to believe that she was stupid. It was strange to me because while she was getting the **B** grade or the **A** grade, I was struggling to get a **C** grade. I was happy that my semester results had improved greatly from what I had in my first year. I believed she was one of the smartest girls I had met in college and I wished she was not so hard on herself. It was disturbing to see her wallow in self-pity and say degrading things about herself.

"My parents think I am worthless and I think so too."

The mind is such an incredible resource because whatever we perceive we can achieve. To envision yourself as a powerful being is something out of the ordinary for many. You can change the world with your words. If you set your mind to something, you can achieve it. College was tough, but I was determined to make it out of college and I made up my mind that I was going to finish well.

Why do some people feel that their immediate circumstances determine their future or how much they can achieve? Usually that is because we truly believe that we are bound by the circumstances we were born into, so we readily accept that we are not able to accomplish our dreams. I have realized that whatever you tell yourself whatever your inner being digests is what will modulate your mind. Why do you think athletes have such discipline to work out every day and put so much effort into their exercises so that they may aspire to be the best in their sport? It is all mindset when we decide that nothing can stop us and no amount of distractions or setbacks can deter us from what we set out to do or what life has in store for each of us. Remember we are all put here on earth for a purpose. Would you not want to find out what that purpose is? Well many of us do not know what our purpose on this earth is. When we pray maybe we have never received the answers to the questions we have been asking so we think our prayers are not being answered, but our prayers are answered because once we get a strong gut feeling about doing something this is a strong spiritual indication.

Also, we often neglect the fact that God has already placed our natural talents within us and we are supposed to train those natural talents into skills. The Bible promises us that those gifts/talents will make room for us and take us before Kings. So, look out for the things that come naturally to you and that you enjoy doing all the time, especially when you are feeling down. In God's design we are meant to be happy in our occupation which brings us into His purpose.

Grieve

I did not get to see my mother much during my marriage years. We talked over the phone most times and I was so scared to tell her that the man I married was doing terrible things to me and the children. I did not want her to know that I had made a huge mistake because I knew it was going to shatter her. "You will marry a good man just like I did. It is sad that your father left us so early, I really wish the hands of death did not have to snatch him away from us. You would have loved him."

I love the way she spoke about my father. You could tell that she still loved him and a part of her wished that they had more time. She told me fascinating stories about him and how they had met. Hers was like the kind of love stories they showed in movies. They had met on the first day they got into high school and they developed their friendship from there. It was a special bond they had that was nurtured into a flame of love that still burned in her heart.

She was alone for the rest of her life. He died and she could not believe that her love had vanished from the earth. My mother walked around for the rest of her life with intense sorrow in her heart. She tried hard to hide it from me when I was much younger and it worked. However, when I grew older, I started to notice the sorrow in her eyes when she spoke about him, when she ate, or when she just sat down on the couch, her mind drifting to the unknown. I thought that she should have moved on in all those years and remarried; maybe she would have been so much happier.

In my third year of college, I experienced what it felt like to lose someone you dearly loved. I still worked two jobs and I still had to support my children and I was doing well in school. I got a call from someone strange one early morning and it was the phone call that broke me.

I replied with a tired, crackly voice that morning. "Hello?"
The voice on the other end was unrecognizable. I had wondered why a strange person would call at that hour. There was a long period of silence on the phone and it made me scared. There was something about the silence that made cold fear resonate within me. The voice on the other end had not said anything, but I knew that something was wrong. Then the voice finally spoke. "You are Karen?"
"Yes, I am." I answered.
"I am Doctor Adam West from Cleveland Clinic. I am sorry to let you know that your mom passed away an hour ago."

I still remember the sound and texture of his voice. It was calm and soothing and I could tell from the way he said it, that he had tried everything in his power to help my mom. I broke down in tears and I cried. I had not cried in a long time like that. I curled up on the floor and cried until I could no longer cry. I shut my eyes to sleep but sleep was so far away. Was that how she felt when she lost my father? Life is somewhat unfair. We cannot be with our loved ones forever and it scares me. One day I will sleep and I will not wake up and my boys will be all alone in the world. Or I may get knocked over by a bus. Or, could it be that I lose my boys? This uncertainty about life gives me unending fear. I have lost the only person that had ever believed in me from birth and I wish she was still alive to read this book.

If I can turn back the hands of time and answer the question I was asked back in college, "How do you do it?" I would say, "My mother." Nobody has ever loved me the way she did. It was the both of us against the world; and I saw my mother struggle daily to provide and care for me. It still hurts me that I made the mistake I made. I wish I could go back to when I was nineteen. I would have loved to have done things differently. My mother is my inspiration and she makes me want to be a better version of myself every single day.

When I turned forty, I got a call from Cheryl. My ex-husband's divorce lawyer had told Cheryl that my ex-husband had died in a car accident. There was not much to be said as I did not know how to feel. We were seated around a table having lunch with Mellissa and Barbara. "He got a stroke while driving and he ran into a truck. His girlfriend was in the car with him. They both died."

The father of my children was dead and I did not know how to feel. The boys were expressionless when I told them he was dead. They did not have any relationship with him and they could not remember all the pain he put us through. Whenever they asked about him, I always told them the truth. "He beat us and he would have killed us, so I left. He is your father and I will not stop you from knowing who he is, but that would be when you are much older to take care of yourself. You cannot meet him as a young boy now, he could take advantage of you." I told them.

Time Is a Wonderful Blessing
The concept of time is very beautiful. When I was younger, I used to think that time was abundant and I could do anything I wanted. As I got older, I realized that time flies and moves too quickly. Death traumatizes you, even now I am yet to recover from the loss of my mother. I have learned to carry on with my life in spite of my heart

being so heavy with sorrow. They say time heals every wound and I am hoping mine will get healed.

Graduating College
College eventually came to an end. It was a hard ride but I was able to finish well. The challenges were there but I did not back out. Nobody has life figured out because life has a way of surprising us. We think we have everything figured and boom! Life happens! The God factor should not be thrown away in our lives because we need Him. Take whatever challenges you have to God because He will answer you.

When I started my college journey, it seemed so far away, it felt like I was never going to reach the finish line; I panicked. I remember calling Cheryl over the phone and we prayed together and we had a long conversation about life in general. She said that it was okay to panic but I needed to know when to stop. If you pray about it, then you leave it with God.

It's Not Always Easy
I gave myself a birthday present on my thirtieth birthday. Cheryl had helped me get one of the prominent divorce lawyers in Miami and he had helped me win my case against my ex-husband. It took me four years and a few months to finally break off from him. He did not want to sign the divorce papers and it is funny because he had somebody else with him. So why did he refuse to sign it? He was mad that I was able to break free from him. He was mad that I left him and he did not get the choice to leave me. I guess it was a blow to his ego. I remember after going through my horrible divorce at a very young age, I was on the Highway driving by a school. Considering that I had recently graduated from college with a Business degree and just started working at a successful cruise line in Miami, Florida, I was

not looking to go back to school at this particular time. Strangely, upon passing this school I had a strong urge to stop by just to inquire about their curriculum and what they had to offer. Following my 'gut feeling' [remember that] I decided to go in. Upon entering I realized that it was a Medical facility and I remember going in very apprehensively because I never thought of working in a hospital and the thought of dealing with blood made my stomach churn. I always knew however that I wanted to do something to help others and so after long hours speaking to the faculty and advisors, I ended up enrolling in classes and I started my career in the medical field as a Radiology nurse. I never knew that I was going to work in the medical field. Now, I have the things I have always wanted. I have two grown adults who are thriving in their own fields. Robert is an engineer in a reputable company in the USA while William and I run a successful business. My writing career is taking off and I am grateful to God for keeping me this long in order to achieve all my desires.

EPILOGUE

There is always an inner voice within us, a 'gut feeling' which we always need to listen to especially in questionable times. Have you heard the words, 'Trust your gut?' Learn to listen to your heart and you will thrive! It is how God speaks to our inner being to guide and protect us.

Fast forward to what is happening today in 2020, there is a global pandemic, a chaotic situation, folks are very apprehensive and the economic situation is in dire need of a revamp. This will soon pass and we should not be frightened. Many people have lost their jobs and businesses and they were made to start again from scratch. Many lost their loved ones and are yet to recover from it. I met a seventy year old woman who lost her husband to the virus and she had been struggling to cope with the fact that she was never going to see her husband of fifty years again.

Our Struggles Are A Part of Our Success Story
Falling behind shouldn't deter you from moving forward. A little setback here and there shouldn't be the reason why you haven't realized your goals. Treat every disappointment as motivation that should steer you towards achieving your goals. Despite the fear and embarrassment that comes with failing, don't give up! Everyone has experienced failure at one point in their lives; remember that you're not the first! Although failure is unpleasant, it is inevitable. It is what comes after the failure that is important. It is your attitude towards handling failure that counts. Your reaction to failure will determine your direction in life. Approach failure differently. Treat failures like stepping stones leading you closer to your dreams and aspirations.
Learn from past mistakes and develop strength in all areas. Don't neglect your physical and mental needs. Learn from your mistakes and watch yourself grow into a strong person. For every failure

you get, encourage yourself to do better. Discouragement isn't the bedrock of any successful person. Successful people recognize discouragement and do away with it quickly. Discouragement feeds off your mental health; it drains you and makes you feel mentally depressed. It fuels the mind with negative emotions. It makes you question yourself and it stampedes on your self-esteem. For every failure that comes your way, don't be discouraged!

Whenever you feel that things aren't going the way you expected, sit back, take a deep breath and relax. It's a common saying that 'good things don't come easy.' Sometimes you need to apply more effort to get the 'good things' that you want. Your determination should be your driving force. Understanding what success entails will make you know what steps to take in the long run. Don't be scared of failure. Failure shouldn't be the reason why you lose hope. There are always challenges and hurdles that you will have to face to become successful. These challenges could be people, laws, etc. Keep in mind that progress might not happen as fast as you want it to; pace yourself.

There are no shortcuts to success. Observation is key when it comes to obtaining success. Sometimes you will need to re-examine your strategy and adopt a new one. Pay close attention to your environment and develop ways that you can harness the things around you. Take notes from successful people to learn from them so that you will not have to make those mistakes that they have made. Learning from others is a significant part of your journey. You will need others to be able to make it in this world. Recognize the people who are significant to your journey and weed out those that are only out to see you fail.

Smartness and success are two peas in a pod. You have to be smart enough to be able to recognize opportunities and take advantage of them. Success in life is subjective and it isn't easy to measure, focus on your goals and do not compare yourself to others. Either way, you still need to be smart. The proper strategy is required in order to achieve what you are aiming for. What worked for someone else may not likely work for you. Understand yourself and the situation around you. The key is to be intelligent enough to know what works for you and honest enough with yourself to choose that route.

Measuring your success with others is not a wise thing to do. Your race on earth is not the same as any other persons' race on earth. Everybody has a unique purpose on earth and it would be a foolish thing to use others as a yardstick to determine where you are going in life. Focus on developing yourself. Comparing yourself with others will only set you up for failure.
You are a woman! A queen! Do not let anyone dim your light!

Finally, dear reader, I sincerely hope that you have come to realize that we all have been through turbulent times in our lives but if you keep your faith and believe in yourself you are able to overcome any obstacle. As a woman and a single mother I was able to realize that I had to break down my obstacles into small goals and regain control of my life. I got through this with prayer and a strong belief that I could do anything I made up my mind to do. This book was written to show other single parents that they too can become successful if they have faith, patience and resilience and I believe we all have a chance to become better and enhance the quality of our lives if we focus on a commitment to excellence.

I decided last year (2021) to start my own business, my own consulting company and I realized that once one takes that first step towards chasing their dream everything else will follow. I have been chosen to speak in the **2022 Success Fest** and I also spoke on the panel of **Becoming the Best You** televised to a million viewers all over the world. I am now adding another title, which is author, to my resume and I am very excited about what the future holds for me. Therefore I look forward to this new chapter of my life with enthusiasm and vigor.

This is only the beginning and I leave my favorite quote with you, **"What you believe you can achieve!"**

ABOUT THE AUTHOR

Karen N. Vaughn is from the Caribbean and grew up in New York and South Florida. This book 'The Essence of a Woman', marks her debut as an author.

A Healthcare professional with an extensive medical background, she has worked in several trauma hospitals including Broward Health and Alameda Hospital in Northern California. She currently works for a Florida, non-profit organization which is affiliated with the Greater Fort Lauderdale Chamber of Commerce.

Karen holds a Bachelor's degree in Marketing Management from Florida Metropolitan University and is currently completing a master's degree from Phoenix University in Mental Health. She also possesses a Diagnostic Medical Sonography degree and currently travels around the United States in her medical practice.

Recently, transitioning into a marketing and public relations extraordinaire, in July of 2020 she formed 'LLC Kay V Connect', a consulting marketing company. In that capacity, she spoke on the 'Success Fest 2021' platform and was a panelist on the 'Becoming the Best You' in November 2021.

Karen strives to keep motivating and making a difference in her community and eventually the world. Her motto in life is, 'All our dreams can come true if we have the courage to pursue them.'

www.ingramcontent.com/pod-product-compliance
Lightning Source LLC
Chambersburg PA
CBHW070942080526
44589CB00013B/1611